It Changes Everything

Published by Mark Gyde

First Published in Great Britain in 2019.

Cover design by Rich Tervet
Cover photograph © Mark Gyde

British Library Cataloguing in Publication Data

ISBN: 978-0-9567792-9-8

It Changes Everything

As I have written this book, I've been very aware that our lives are a journey. For much of this journey we travel alone as it's a journey of our heart. However, I am also aware that this journey is one with friends. To list them all would take a lot of time and I would be sure to miss some out. But, from the bottom of my heart, I say 'thank you' to you all.

Of course, there are some people who need special thanks and they are my wife, Fiona, and my family: Frances and Rich, Hilary, Hannah, and John. Without you the journey wouldn't have been so much fun and I would have missed out on the joy of being loved. Thank you!

CONTENTS

FOREWORD

I've been privileged to have been part of Mark Gyde's journey for the last eighteen years or so. I am proud to be part of his life and to have him as a friend. He is a man that God has put His hand on to be a witness to the world of who He is.

As Mark explains, our hearts are where we meet with God and God's aim has never been for us to knuckle down and obey a long list of requirements. Instead our response of love to Him supersedes mere obedience. In the Old Testament God says 'obedience is better than sacrifice' but the New Testament reveals that love has to be the engine of obedience, 'if you love me you will keep my word' (John 14:15).

The difference between obeying someone powerful who says "we must" is a Grand Canyon away from fulfilling the desire of someone we love. What an empty life it would be if my wife and I only served each other from cold obedience rather than from a love that wants to see each other's lives enhanced with increasing joy.

Today many people live what they call a Christian life but in reality, it has a deep root in Old Testament principle and lifestyle. 'Right thinking' is deemed to be faith, leading to the correct action, which then becomes the focus of a successful Christian walk. Righteousness is then assessed on whether we sin or not (the absence of a negative) rather than on the love of God (the possession of a positive). Normal Christian life is wrapped in the love of God. It is quietly, solidly, stable in the certainty of God's approval which we can then bring to those around us.

In God's agenda, we are now in a season where light is being shone all over the world on the love of God as Father. In the past it has shone on who Jesus is and what He has done. It has shone on who the Holy Spirit is and what He will do. But now we are in a time when the Father is pouring His love into our hearts.

Mark Gyde is at the forefront of this outpouring of the Father's love and of the greater revelation of biblical truth which it leads us to imbibe. "Love changes everything" – how true and how wonderful!

M. James Jordan

It Changes Everything

Chapter One

Fatherheart of God

In 1995 I went to Uganda for the first time. I was helping to lead a team of teenagers from the school which was linked to our church. It was an incredible, eye opening experience. I'd seen a lot of TV news about Africa which showed the poverty and a very different way of life to the one I was used to. But there is something very different to seeing it on a TV screen and actually being there as part of the story. Standing in the middle of a street in a city where there was hardly any electricity, little by way of clean water and even less in terms of healthy sanitation.

We'd left Heathrow at lunchtime the day before and, because of the necessity of obtaining cheap tickets, we'd flown through various middle eastern countries. The airplane acted more like a local bus service than an international flight as there were several stops not noted on our flight itinerary. After nearly twenty four hours we landed at Entebbe where a school lorry was waiting to take us to Kasana Children's Centre (New Hope Uganda), the children's home and orphanage we'd come to visit. In theory it should have been a two and a half hour journey. But….. on the way from Entebbe to Kampala the lorry driver suddenly pulled off the road and drove through the bush (literally, I don't even recall there being a track) as he wanted to visit his family who lived in a local village. Then we needed to stop in Kampala, at Shop

7

10, to stock up on provisions for the next two weeks. Finally, we started the journey and I experienced every pothole and bump very acutely.

I think for the whole journey I had my mouth wide open as this was something that I'd never experienced before. It was wonderful. I have to say that over the past twenty or so years the experience has changed; the roads are better, the airport is better, communication is better. In 1995, I had to travel two hours to Kampala, hope the fax machine was working and hope the electricity was on in order to send my daughter a birthday message. Now I can easily send texts or have decent phone conversations simply by using my mobile phone. Nonetheless the thrill and delight of traveling to Uganda is unchanged.

As we pulled off the 'main' road into the children's centre I saw the welcoming sign: *"A Father to the fatherless, a defender of widows, is God in his holy dwelling. God sets the lonely in families"* (Psalm 68:5-6). And this was followed by: "Bringing the Fatherheart of God to the fatherless".

Over the next few days, time and time again, I was hit by the impact of those statements. As I walked round the site I saw the homes that had been built, orphaned children being taken into families and the love of God, the Father, being expressed in a way I'd not previously seen. Here children who had nothing, who'd lost everything, were being given a home, security, value, identity but most importantly they were discovering love. They were being loved. Not only the love of human affection but the powerful, life changing love of the perfect Father. They were discovering that God was real, that he was not distant or angry but he was longing to hold these children in his arms of love and to be a Father to them.

Throughout my three weeks at Kasana I saw love in action. Sometimes I would look into the children's eyes and see the emptiness that came from all the pain of their young lives, the brokenness of having parents snatched away through sickness or death. In other children, that emptiness was starting to fade as a small sparkle of life could begin to be seen in their eyes. In every case, though, there was hope. There was hope because here was a place, a family, where the love of the Father was being poured into hearts that desperately needed it. These children had been brought into a hostile world and had suffered the biggest loss imaginable, the loss of parents, family and home. They had become orphans. Instead of a secure life they had begun to live in fear, very often for their own survival.

But at Kasana they found a place where love began to drive out the fear of their empty orphan hearts. Here was a love that was beginning to transform lives.

This was only possible because the staff and carers at New Hope Uganda had discovered this love for themselves. As they received love, they could pass it on.

9

That trip, in 1995, was before the advent of digital photography and so I rationed myself to ten rolls of film for my time away. Even so, the photos don't do justice to what was actually happening there or what I was experiencing. It was so unlike watching the news on TV; being there I actually became part of the story, part of the events that were taking place each and every day. Part of the frustration of not having electricity or running water all the time, the hassle of pumping and filtering water before it could be used, the constant struggles with health and sanitation. I was there, I was in it. It was not several thousands of miles away, being captured on TV cameras and then beamed into the comfort of my living room in the UK.

In the same way I witnessed the Fatherheart of God. As John writes at the start of his first letter, I saw it, I touched it, I experienced it. Here was a living demonstration of the love of the Father in practice. It was real and in many practical ways was touching and changing people's lives.

Many years earlier I'd read Floyd McClung's book 'The Father Heart of God'. I'm sure many of you have read the story of him working with the prostitutes in the red light district of Amsterdam. As Floyd and his team worked with some of the most rejected and broken people in society they did so with one aim: to show them that they were precious to Almighty God, that he loved and valued them and that, despite and because of their brokenness, he wanted to be a Father to them.

10

It is the same heart being shown to prostitutes in Amsterdam as to the orphans in Uganda. It is the heart of the perfect Father who has never lost sight of his desire to bring his sons and daughters home, to bring them back from their rebellion and to give them their rightful place in the family. The cry in God's heart has always been and will always be '*I thought you would call me Father!*' (Jeremiah 3:19).

Before I move on to look at what the Fatherheart of God is, I want to mention a couple of other events in my own journey. Both have become part of the foundation of God being a Father to me.

Shortly after leaving school, I was on a youth holiday arranged by our group of churches. We were staying at a hotel in the Lake District and during the days we would go off walking or exploring the beautiful countryside. In the evenings we met together in the hotel for other social activities and on the last night for a time of worship and teaching. At the end of the meeting, just as I was gathering my stuff together one of the leaders, Dave Richards, came over to me and knelt on the floor in front of me. He said one simple sentence which brought a seismic shift in my heart. All he said was, 'Mark, you've learned to be a servant, but God wants you to be a son'. I knew then, in that moment, that God was my Father. I knew I was a son.

That simple sentence changed me and I believe started me on this journey of living loved and allowing God to be a Father to me.

Never underestimate the power of simple, chance encounters like that. I believe if our heart is open then the Father can and will speak to us. As we listen, we are changed, not so much by the actual words themselves but by the source of love behind the words. Love always transforms.

I've often asked myself, 'why me?'. Why did Dave Richards say those words to me? More importantly why did Father say those words to me? I don't remember feeling particularly spiritual on that evening, what I really wanted to do was put my stuff away and go to the bar for a drink with my friends. I didn't really think about having an open heart or hearing the voice of the Father. But yet he spoke those words into my heart and I was changed.

I trust that we may all hear these words, 'you've learned to be a servant, but I want you to be my son or my daughter'. As we hear them, they will change our lives.

The second event was many years later in December 1996. At that time we were having weekly meetings where we saw the Holy Spirit do many exciting things. One week we had Gerald Coates coming to speak. Gerald is a very entertaining speaker as well as carrying an anointing of the Holy Spirit. However, as the evening wore on I became more and more disappointed. The worship had not been great, what Gerald shared was not particularly inspiring and then he said there wouldn't be a ministry time. I was beginning to wish I'd stayed at home for the evening.

relationship with our Father and it is him enjoying his relationship with us, his children. After all, parents enjoy their children and those same children delight in being with their mum and dad. Over Christmas, I've watched my eighteen month old grandson with his parents. Of course, there are times when he is tired and wants to be fed or put to bed but there are many other times when he giggles uncontrollably as his mum and dad play with him. It's contagious seeing that type of pleasure. We love a good time of worship or our devotional times, it is in those times that we delight in our relationship with our Heavenly Father, we feel close to him. How much more does he delight in us. *"I will rejoice in doing them good and will assuredly plant them in this land with all my heart and soul"* (Jeremiah 32:41). Can you imagine what something looks like when God does it with **all** his heart and soul, there is a lot of joy in his heart which is expressed towards us.

As we come to know his heart, we discover the care and compassion he has for us. We experience his affection and affirmation, we feel his presence with us and his pleasure towards us. We find that God has a heart and that his heart is turned towards his people rather than being set against them.

The problem is that we are so conditioned by our experience of earthly fathers that we often miss the point. We don't know what pure love is because we have only experienced love with conditions. Experiencing love, of any kind, becomes like an on/off switch; dependent on us, on others or on our circumstances.

When you know someone's heart you feel as if you are beginning to know the real them. As we talk about the Fatherheart of God, I believe we are beginning to seek or desire something more in our relationship with him.

One of the joys I have is being able to speak at various schools of ministry. I'm invited to do the 'Fatherheart' module, something I love doing. A frustration I often have is that a few days is too short. (This can also be the case with our Fatherheart schools). I can point people towards something, I can help people through some of the blockages to knowing God as Father. I can hope they experience something but I'm often left with a question: have they got it? Maybe, they too, have the same question: 'have I got it'?

What is 'it'?

We were made to enjoy a relationship with God as Father and this has been stolen from us. We were born again to enjoy a life far beyond what many of us experience, beyond what has sadly become the norm. Jesus came to give us life and life in all its fulness (John 10:10), where is that life, how have we lost sight of it?

Knowing about the Fatherheart of God is a start. It's the beginning of our heart being awakened to the truth of who we really are, and who he really is. We're seeking, or longing, for something more; our heart is yearning to know God in the same way as we see Jesus knowing him throughout the gospels. Something is coming alive. But knowing 'about' is not the 'it' that I'm talking about. The

In Romans 10:10 we read, *"For it is with your heart that you believe and are justified, and it is with your mouth that you profess your faith and are saved."* Our heart deals with issues of belief and conscience, the real issues of right and wrong. The Holy Spirit speaks to our heart, he whispers to us, he leads us by gently tugging at cords of loving kindness which are attached to our heart (Hosea 11:4).

In this book I don't want to criticise but I do want to provoke.

I imagine that you are reading this book because you want something to change. The title has drawn you in and that means you are dissatisfied with how things are for you at the moment. You are interested in what 'it' is and what sort of change you can begin to dream of. No, not dream of, but the change you can actually experience. If you desire change you must, by definition, be fed up (to some extent) with how things currently are. You want change, maybe you're desperate for change. I believe you've picked up this book because you yearn for change and you want your life to be different. I'm not intending to criticise where you are presently at on your journey, nor am I criticising your background or your journey thus far. But I do want to provoke you to believe that change is possible.

I'm not inviting you into a theological argument. I'm not inviting you to struggle with these issues in your mind but I am inviting you along the pathway of transformation and, what really needs to change is our heart. We cannot make ourselves change, we can try and it may last for a day, a week or maybe even a month. Any change that has been made by a decision of our mind can be reversed should we start to think or believe something different. What the Father does in our heart will lead to a permanent transformation as it is done by him, not us. He does not take back that which he has given.

Even as we begin to consider thinking with our heart, I hear some of you say 'ah but, the heart is weak, evil beyond repair, how can we trust our heart?'(Jeremiah 17:9). I'm not asking you to trust your heart, I'm asking you to trust what Father does in your heart. Whatever the state of your heart, whatever is going on in your life, the Father has chosen to make his home there (John 14:23). That is an amazing truth and one we can hang onto however desperate we may feel. He knows the true state of our heart, yet he voluntarily chooses to live there. We know our heart and often wonder why he would do such a thing. He does it because he is God and he is not afraid of, or put off by, mess. In fact, I think he prefers mess to what we try and make neat and tidy.

The change we long to experience is a transformation of our heart and this, in due course, will lead to a transformation of our mind (Romans 12:2). The life of God flows from within us, it is the spring of living water that starts in our heart. First of all it changes us. Then it flows out from us to others and will ultimately reach and touch this broken world around us (John 4:14 and John 7:38). The life of God finds its source in our heart, it is

24

not the result of us changing our mind and deciding to live differently. I don't like it when people say we have to be 'intentional' about something or another. That implies we could subsequently change our mind and be intentional about something else. When our heart is changed we will automatically live differently, not because we choose to but because we want to. The Father's own Spirit, dwelling in our heart, will cause (or motivate) us to walk in his ways (Ezekiel 36:27).

As you read on, think with your heart. It is with your heart you believe and are saved. Thinking with your heart will lead you into a transformed life.

I wonder whether you think your heart is in prison. Very often that's the way we feel when we are longing for a change of heart or desiring something more. It's like we're in captivity and we're longing for freedom.

This is what Jeremiah had to say.

*"For I know the plans I have for you," declares the Lord, "plans to prosper you and not to harm you, plans to give you hope and a future. Then you will call on me and come and pray to me, and I will listen to you. You will seek me and find me **when you seek me with all your heart**. I will be found by you," declares the Lord, "and will bring you back from captivity. I will gather you from all the nations and places where I have banished you," declares the Lord, "and will bring you back to the place from which I carried you into exile."* (Jeremiah 29:11-14)

Here is a promise. God will **always** be found by us when we seek him with **all** of our heart. I love understanding the Bible from a theological point of view, I enjoy the history and even the original Greek or Hebrew meaning of words. They are fascinating, they enable me to present things more clearly but they are not the things which change my heart. Finding him is what changes my heart.

For us to discover the 'it', the thing that will change everything, we must give ourselves permission to go on a journey. We need to leave the place where we have settled and become discontent and then set out to follow the yearning in our heart for something more.

There was an occasion when the disciples asked Jesus why he spoke to the people in parables (Matthew 13:10-17). Jesus' reply is not a direct answer to their question, instead he tells them that **they** are the ones who have been given an understanding of the Kingdom of Heaven. The crowds see but don't perceive, they hear but don't understand. In other words, unlike the disciples, the crowds are not thinking with their heart. They are trying to grapple with something in their mind and it is not bringing them clarity or understanding. The reason for this lack of clarity is because their hearts have become hardened, or closed. They can't see the truth, as it is only the eyes of the heart that can really see and understand and their eyes were closed. The crowds were spiritually blind.

decision. What then do we do? At such times it's easy to let our shame and condemnation prevent us from turning and seeking to rediscover the pathway of life. But it is possible. It's possible because love always gives us a choice and it will always provide a way for us to come back home to Father. There will always be an opportunity to return and once again we can fall into the everlasting arms of the Father who does not judge or condemn.

When we've made a bad decision we tend to beat ourselves up and send ourselves into a period of self-imposed exile. We believe that if we punish ourselves, we can make our own self-righteous way back to God. It doesn't work as the way back has already been given to us; it's of his making, not ours.

When Jesus offered us life and life in its fulness, he wasn't offering us a different lifestyle to the one he lived. Despite the clashes with the Pharisees and the Romans, Jesus lived life to the full because the thing that defined it for him was an intimacy of relationship with his Father. For us, when we walk as Jesus walked, we will also discover this fulness of life.

Knowing God as Father is to know him in the same way as Jesus knows him. It is much more than knowing *about* him, it is a heart relationship where we know his personality and nature, where we really know what he thinks about us and where we begin to trust him with our whole heart.

31

What is 'it'?

Even the title of this chapter can be a bit ambiguous, 'Knowing God as Father'. What is the knowing that I'm talking about? I hope you have seen, as you've been reading, that it is not the processing of information or the understanding of theology. It is allowing him to fully make his home in your heart, and, as he does, you begin to truly know him for who he really is. Of course, he knows everything about us (all of the time) but there is something more mysterious which happens when we know he is dwelling in our heart. Not only do we know him, but maybe for the first time in our life we begin to feel that we too, are known.

What is really going to make the difference and bring the change we are pursuing? I believe it is when we come to know that God is a Father to us. Those two words, 'to us' make so much difference. They don't describe a formal, business-like relationship but rather a life-giving and life-changing one. Knowing God as Father is not simply knowing that he is a father, it is experiencing him being a Father to us and this is something I'll explore in chapter four.

Chapter Three

The Revelation of God as Father

A revelation occurs when something that has been hidden is revealed. It is an enlightening experience that enables us to grasp something that we either didn't know anything about or have struggled to understand.

A revelation makes something that was complex into something so blindingly obvious. So much so that we often ask 'how have I missed this up to now?' Instead of stumbling around in the dark, light comes and everything becomes clear.

I am going to paint a very clear picture of how the Father is revealed through scripture. Again, I ask you to see this with the eyes of your heart, let the Holy Spirit be a light to your path and a lamp to your feet (Psalm 119:105). God as Father is not something new but is merely stating what has always been, even from before the beginning of time. God does not change, he is the same yesterday, today and tomorrow. He didn't suddenly become Father when Jesus came to earth, he didn't have a change of heart between Malachi and Matthew, it wasn't his latest idea to try and win us over. He has always been Father and always will be Father – the question that we are faced with is, will we let him be a Father to us?

I will look at John 17 in more detail later in the chapter but for now, let me highlight one thing Jesus says:

"Father, I want those you have given me to be with me where I am, and to see my glory, the glory you have given me because you loved me before the creation of the world." (John 17:24)

This describes the Father/Son relationship that has existed for all eternity. It's one of intimacy, honour and love. As we will see later, this relationship was to be shared just as earthly parents want to share and extend their love for one another by having children. It's natural to want a family because we're made in the image of God and that's what he's always wanted. Rebellion and disobedience don't put him off; he does everything to bring his children back home into the family.

The words 'in the beginning' are used twice in the bible; once at the start of Genesis and once at the start of John's gospel. They are not in chronological order as the first 'in the beginning' is the one in John 1:1 where John describes what it was like in the time before the clock started ticking in Genesis. In the beginning before the beginning there was a relationship, a Father and a Son. In simple terms, the Son came to earth to become the way for us to come back to the Father. It is as we believe in the Son that we are given the right to become children of the Father. This is the only way that our salvation is possible. Knowing Jesus, however wonderful that is (and it is), was never meant to be an end in itself. It was always intended to be doorway into something greater and that is to become children of Almighty God.

The second 'in the beginning' was the start of God's family plan. He made a beautiful home, called planet earth, a place for us live. He filled it with beauty and mystery, he made it big enough and complex enough for us to explore and discover. And finally, he made us, in his image with the intention of us enjoying him forever.

Sadly, it doesn't take many pages of the story before everything has gone badly wrong. We discover the story has a villain who is out to destroy everything that has been created and he does it swiftly and devastatingly. Despite mankind turning its back on God and choosing to pursue independence, God does not reject his people, he does not reject us.

Even as he drives Adam and Eve out of the garden we see the hand of a loving Father at work. We see a Father who has pity on his children as they start to walk out of the garden covered in fig leaves. I think that breaks his heart, so he kills an animal and makes clothes to cover and protect his children. A simple, yet powerful act of a loving Father. He then protects them from eating from the tree of life and therefore being able to live forever in a fallen separated state.

What follows is not a story of judgement or rejection of the very people he has created. What follows is the most powerful love story of all time where a father pursues his children, doing everything he can to provide a way for them to come back home. Jesus tells us in John 8:35-36 that sons (and daughters) belong to the family forever. At no point in history has God, the Father, ever stopped being a Father and therefore at no point in history has he cast us out of his family. When we come to Son, Jesus, we are set free. Set free not only from the power of sin, but set free to live as sons and daughters. Whenever we are set free, we are always set free from something in order to be free to become someone. If we don't see that there are these two parts to our freedom we will not fully enter the freedom that is offered to us.

The whole of the Old Testament is very simple; it's the story of a Father who has lost his kids and does anything and everything to win them back again. Everything else is a sub-story and not the main narrative.

We cannot fail to see the Fatherheart of God throughout the Old Testament scriptures. To highlight what I mean let me list a few, I have added some emphasis to highlight this continual narrative.

"They are corrupt and not his children; to their shame they are a warped and crooked generation. Is this the way you repay the Lord, you foolish and unwise people? Is he not your Father, your Creator, who made you and formed you?" (Deuteronomy 32:5-6)

"You deserted the Rock, who fathered you; you forgot the God who gave you birth." (Deuteronomy 32:18)

"Hear me, you heavens! Listen, earth! For the Lord has spoken: "I reared children and brought them up, but they have rebelled against me." (Isaiah 1:2)

"When Israel was a child, I loved him, and out of Egypt I called my son. But the more they were called, the more they went away from me. They sacrificed to the Baals and they burned incense to images. It was I who taught Ephraim to walk, taking them by the arms; but they did not realize it was I who healed them. I led them with cords of human kindness, with ties of love. To them I was like one who lifts a little child to the cheek, and I bent down to feed them." (Hosea 11:1-4)

*"But now, this is what the Lord says: he who created you, Jacob, he who formed you, Israel: "Do not fear, for I have redeemed you; I have **called you by name**; you are mine. When you pass through the waters, I will be with you; and when you pass through the rivers, they will not sweep over you. When you walk through the fire, you will not be burned; the flames will not set you ablaze.*
*I will say to the north, 'Give them up!' and to the south, 'Do not hold them back.' **Bring my sons from afar and my daughters from the ends of the earth**, everyone who is called by my name, whom I created for my glory, whom I formed and made."* (Isaiah 43:1-2, 6-7)

Nowhere do we see the heart of the Father more clearly than in Jeremiah 3:19.

"I myself said, 'How gladly would I treat you like sons and give you a pleasant land, the most beautiful inheritance of any nation. I thought you would call me 'Father' and not turn away from following me.'"

This one verse contains the Father's longing – *'how gladly would I treat you like sons'*. It contains a promise of blessing – *'give you a pleasant land'*. A promise of inheritance and generosity – *'the most beautiful inheritance of any nation'*. But most of all it contains the Father's ultimate desire – *'I thought you would call me Father'*. It couldn't be any clearer. God wants to be called 'Father' because that's who he is. A father gives his children a blessing and an inheritance which goes way beyond anything a master would give to his servants.

I've just selected a few verses from the Old Testament, there are many, many more. The story that runs through the first thirty nine books of the Bible is not a theology of God being a Father but a descriptive revelation of who he is.

As I look at what our Father is like I'm going to delve into one passage of scripture in some detail. John 17 is Jesus' final prayer before is he led away to the cross. In this prayer, he is seemingly giving an account of his time on earth to his Father. It reads a bit like the fulfilment of a mission statement: this is what you sent me to do and this is what I have done.

There are many times throughout John's gospel, in particular, where Jesus refers to his total commitment to do the Father's will and work. His whole life, even as a twelve year old boy, was to seek his Father's will and then do it will all of his heart. It was his sole focus, but it was more than that, it was his sole passion.

Jesus starts his prayer by showing that our eternal life is not just dependent on us knowing him, but it centres around us knowing the Father as well. Again, this is an area where we settle for less than we should. All too often we make our eternal life Jesus centred. Yes, he is the source of our salvation and our redemption is found in him. Our eternal life starts, not when we go to Heaven, but when we come to him and believe in him as our Lord and Saviour. But eternal life is bigger than all these things. Jesus says, *"now this is eternal life: that they know **you (the Father)**, the only true God, and Jesus Christ, whom you have sent"* (John 17:3). Eternal life is centred around the Father because that's who the Son leads us to. Jesus does not draw people to himself but he draws us and takes us to the Father.

As his prayer progresses, Jesus says these words, *'I have revealed you'* (v6). Another translation says, *"I have made your name known"* and this is a statement that is rich in meaning. This is much more than a formal introduction or a handshake. Jesus is saying that he has revealed the full nature and personality of his Father, he has shown us what God is really like. Moses was given a glimpse of what God was like when he asked to see his glory (Exodus 33:18). He saw a glimpse of what we can see and experience fully. As Moses is on the mountain the presence of God comes down in a cloud and stands next to him. God announces his name and then reveals his character.

"The Lord, the Lord, the compassionate and gracious God, slow to anger, abounding in love and faithfulness,

maintaining love to thousands, and forgiving wickedness, rebellion and sin. Yet he does not leave the guilty unpunished; he punishes the children and their children for the sin of the parents to the third and fourth generation." (Exodus 34:6-7)

Why do we spend so long dwelling on the second part of these verses as we think of punishment and sin? That's not the nature of our Father, it's the consequence of ignoring him and leaving him out of our life. He is loving. He is gracious. He is faithful and forgiving. Very similar, in fact, to the fruit of the Spirit.

"But the fruit of the Spirit is love, joy, peace, forbearance, kindness, goodness, faithfulness, gentleness and self-control. Against such things there is no law." (Galatians 5:22)

In our understanding of the Father we seem to ignore these qualities and make up our own lists which contain false and misleading attributes. The bible is clear; God is LOVE and not anything else we try and make him to be. As we live in love, the fruit of the Spirit will grow in us as his divine nature becomes the source of our daily life. Knowing him, and living in relationship with him, will produce fruit that reflects his nature and personality.

This is the Father who Jesus revealed because this is the Father Jesus knew. The Father of love, the God of all comfort and the Father of all mercies. Jesus has made the Father clearly known.

40

He then says another significant statement which is also full of meaning: *"I have given them the words you gave me"* (v8). Jesus was, and is, the Word of God. Therefore all the words he spoke were actually the Father's words. In John 8:28 Jesus says he does nothing on his own but only speaks the words that his Father has taught him to say. It's like the script has been rehearsed so everything Jesus does and says leads to the intended purpose of revealing his Father.

As a twelve year old boy, Jesus sits in the temple listening to and questioning the teachers. His time there ends with them asking him questions. We read that the teachers are amazed at his understanding and the answers he is giving. Even at that age, the words he spoke were his Father's words and it's no wonder, therefore, that his listeners were astonished. He was speaking words of life and I believe he was revealing his Father to those around him.

Many years later, Jesus is in the synagogue in his home town of Nazareth and it's his turn to read the scriptures. He is handed the scroll and reads from the prophet Isaiah. For the first time in history the Word of God is reading the word of God. What a poignant moment that would have been. Normally the one who read the scripture would then preach to those who had gathered. Jesus didn't, he simply sat down after saying, 'Today this scripture is fulfilled in your hearing'. It needed no further explanation, what he'd read described himself and there was nothing more to add.

41

There was a time when the crowds moved away from Jesus and stopped following him. He asks his disciples, his closest friends, if they too will be leaving. For Peter, it is obvious, there is nowhere else to go because Jesus 'has the words of eternal life' (John 6:68).

A lot of the things Jesus said were challenging and direct. He certainly said some very direct things to the Pharisees but they seemed unable to listen. Yes, of course, he challenged their religion and their hardness of heart. I believe he did so in order to expose the shallowness and deception of their beliefs. Ultimately, I believe he wanted them to hear words of life just as much as he wanted that for the crowds of ordinary people. The people were desperate and could shake off the shackles of religion and the blind obedience to the law as they found the pathway of life. The Pharisees had become content with their way of life and the control they had over other people. They felt safe, but they had no life.

Whoever Jesus spoke to, he spoke words of life. Some people, like the rich young ruler, couldn't receive them and they went away sad. Even then, we read in Mark 10, Jesus looked at him with eyes of love.

Everything Jesus did and said was to reveal his Father. Not everyone receives or believes it. The words Jesus spoke, and the words he speaks to us today, come straight from the heart of the Father. Just as we sometimes can't see the nature and character of the Father, so we also mis-hear the words of the gospel. Instead of a message of love and freedom from shame

42

and condemnation, we hear a message of good works, of striving and activity. The words we hear don't bring us eternal life because we hear them through a filter, something we'll look at more in the next chapter.

Jesus shows us what his Father is really like, he gives us his words and then shows us that we are able to relate to the Father in same way that the Trinity relates to each other.

"I have given them the glory that you gave me, that they may be one as we are one, I in them and you in me, so that they may be brought to complete unity." (verses 22-23)

As the Father is revealed we discover trinitarian unity, the gift of oneness. One of the things we struggle with is living in unity. It's all too easy to judge or criticise and that always leads to division. As we come to know the Father we are brought into the glory of Jesus, we are enabled to live as he lived. I'll be looking at our relationships in a later chapter, all I want to say now is that the revelation of the Father brings us into unity with him and into unity with one another.

Another thing I'll be looking at in more detail is our traditional belief, or understanding, that being a Christian is all about salvation. That's a major part but it's not the whole story. As Jesus summarises his work on earth, he gives us a glimpse of what the Father has in his mind.

"Father, I want those you have given me to be with me where I am." (verse 24)

Jesus has an overwhelming desire for us to know that we can be with him where he is. He came from the bosom of the Father and has returned there. He is seated at the Father's right hand in the heavenly places (John 1:18 and Ephesians 2:6) and that's where he wants us to join him. He is not just talking about our eternal future but is also addressing how we live our daily life. As we are drawn into love we begin to discover that our true home is with him. He has made his home in our heart and we make our home in his heart. He is in us and we are in him.

Having stated that he has revealed the Father and made him known, Jesus now makes one of the most important statements of his ministry. The last words Jesus speaks before he is led away to the cross really do sum up what his life and ministry have been about. He has already alluded to this in Matthew 11 when he said to his disciples, *"no on knows the Father except the Son and those to whom the Son chooses to reveal him"* (Matthew 11:27). All Jesus wants to do is reveal his Father and now in John 17 he leaves us with a promise that holds true for us just as much as it did for the disciples.

"I have made you known to them, and will continue to make you known...." (v26)

This part of Jesus' prayer is often called the prayer for all believers and that makes it a promise for you and me. As Jesus concludes his earthly ministry he gives us this promise, that he will continue to reveal the Father to us. That is exceptionally good news! It also implies that there is a greater, ongoing revelation for us to experience. What we have received thus far may have been good but there is always more and it will be better than what we've seen and experienced.

But that is not all. In John 17 we have an amazing summary of how Jesus revealed the Father. Jesus has shown us the Father's nature and character, he has given us his word, he enables us to live like the Trinity and he wants us to be with him where he is. We have the promise of a deepening and ongoing journey with Father and finally we hear some words which many of us struggle to believe.

"I have made you known to them, and will continue to make you known in order that the love you have for me may be in them and that I myself may be in them." (v26)

I prefer the wording in the Passion Translation.

"I have revealed to them who you are and I will continue to make you even more real to them, so that they may experience the same endless love that you have for me, for your love will now live in them, even as I live in them!"

These last words of Jesus sum it all up. We are loved by the Father as Jesus is loved. The Father loves you and me in the same way and with the same intensity of passion as he loves his son, Jesus. Please do not move on until you have let those words settle in your heart because as they do you will begin to believe that his love really can change everything.

What is 'it'?

The revelation of God as Father is so we can see who God is. For it to make a difference we need to embrace it, we need a personal encounter of God being a Father to us.

In this chapter I have given a clear biblical overview of the revelation of God as Father. I have dwelt on the specific revelation of the Father through the life of Jesus as recorded in John 17. Now I shall look at how we can receive and embrace this for ourselves.

Chapter Four

A Father to YOU

We have a problem.

We can't see or experience the love of our Heavenly Father because we tend not to have very good examples or role models. However good our parents have been they haven't been perfect. They missed out on perfect love because our grandparents were unable to give them everything they needed. For many people just mentioning the word 'father' brings back too many bad memories: abuse, pain, torment or turmoil. Why would those people want to experience God as Father when the associations are so bad.

Because of our experience we begin to see God through the filter of how our parents were towards us. If our dad or mum was angry, we think God is angry and always ready to jump on us and condemn us for any small failing. When a child is on the receiving end of anger all they want to do is run and hide. Anger exposes our weakness and shortcomings and the last thing we want is for those to be constantly laid bare. An angry response is never a good one because the spoken words are barbed and they sink deeply into a child's heart, causing wounds that can last a lifetime. An angry response can often be physical, and that is never good. The old saying 'sticks and stones may break my bones, but words will never hurt me' is so untrue. Our body might recover from physical abuse but often our heart never recovers from verbal abuse. Either way, verbal or physical, anger creates real wounds and that causes us to hide. Fear settles in our heart and we'll do anything to run and avoid it. Fear might be a response to avoid more pain, but it also starts to make us believe all those negative things which have been said, or done. All that does is to create a life of shame which is so hard to break free from.

Anger can become a filter through which we see God. Something inside of us tells us God is angry with us because we've not done the right thing or we've not done it well enough. As we hide from our earthly parents so we hide from God. The same fear grips us and all we see is an angry God who is out to judge every single action and attitude. We can never be good enough.

Another filter we create comes from parents who are absent. They may be absent through death, divorce or separation. Or they may be absent by being at work for long hours. They may be absent because, despite being in the same room, they're hidden behind a computer, smartphone or the television. An absent father or mother communicates that a child does not matter or that their presence is not important. Absent parents communicate that their children don't have any value. For some of us having absent parents is no particular person's fault, it might just be the cruel way things have worked out. It's not a case of laying blame but being able to recognise that a lack of time or care and attention damages children.

Of course, if we believe that our parents don't value us or want to spend time with us why would we ever believe God would want to? We assume he's not bothered with us and doesn't care about us. Therefore we fall into the habit of being alone and seeing our own strength as the only way we can make a better life for ourselves. In short, we want to be the solution to all our problems.

A father can be controlling or manipulative. Maybe because of their own insecurities they seek to control others. They might even do this because they think they know best and they don't want their children to make unnecessary mistakes. Control stifles freedom and does not allow the other person to determine their own way through life. If we've had controlling or manipulative parents we can easily think that God is just the same, dangling us on a piece of string as if we were a puppet.

A final filter we can create is that of a good father or mother. The problem with this is that we define perfection from our own perspective and this restricts the goodness of God to the goodness of our parents. It brings him down to a human level.

When we have been looking through a filter the only way to see clearly is to remove the filter. Sometimes that's not easy. Sometimes we can't do it on our own, we need help. We need help to begin to see God as he really is, rather than through the filter of our earthly parents. Friends, family, a pastor or a counsellor can all help us deconstruct the filters we've created and begin to help us see more clearly the Father who has been hidden. But there is another gift we can receive to help us remove the filters. It's the gift of faith. Faith is not something we have to work up for ourselves. It's not based on merit but it's a gift (Ephesians 2:8). We can ask for this gift of faith and that will enable us to see an unfiltered view or image of God our Father. We may need to work through the consequences of our filters but faith is the assurance, or reality, of seeing things that have previously been hidden.

All of these filters, which form part of our historical view of God, can be taken away and, as they are, we allow God to be a Father to us. Do not let your history define your future.

In the 1992 Olympic games there was a British athlete, Derek Redmond. He was hopeful of a medal but in the 400m semi-final he tore a hamstring, effectively putting him out of the race. He persevered as he wanted to finish the race even if it meant coming last. As he hobbles on, an older man comes out of the crowd, runs up to him and puts his arm around his shoulders. With the support of the older man Redmond makes it to the finish. He was last, but he finished and his time was recorded.

The older man was his father.

What an example. A father who was prepared to join his son in his pain and apparent failure. A father who stuck with his son through the good times and the not so good times. A father who was prepared to be humiliated alongside his son. In fact, none of that happened. Instead of any shame or humiliation, the crowd in the Olympic stadium stood and gave Derek Redmond and his father a standing ovation and cheered them onto the finish line. No one remembers who won that race but everyone knows who came last. With pride and honour the crowd saluted him over the line.

Our Father is like that, only better. He is with us through thick and thin, through the good and bad, through our successes and failures. He never leaves us nor does he let us down. His love is constant and unimaginably amazing.

As an accountant, I've been in many of my clients' offices. On one occasion I was in a church office and the pastor told me a story of a young man in their town who loved getting girls pregnant. He'd fathered sixteen children but had no ongoing relationship with any of them. He was the father **of** sixteen children, but the father **to** none of them. What a contrast to Derek Redmond's father and how totally incomparable to our Heavenly Father whose desire is to be a Father to us.

It is a fact that this young man was a father, but it was a relationship which showed the world that Derek Redmond's dad was a father. It's not a series of facts or principles that will change us but a relationship.

There is a huge difference between knowing that God is a father and knowing he is a Father to you. One is a piece of information, the other describes a heart relationship.

Let us, therefore, take a look at the Father's love and see how it is much more than a fact or theological truth. We need to begin to experience this love as a tangible substance being poured into our heart.

"See what great love the Father has lavished on us, that we should be called children of God! And that is who we are! The reason the world does not know us is that it did not know him." (1 John 3:1)

Some translations say 'what kind of love' so let's examine it and see what kind of love it is.

Before I start, let me quote this verse again, but this time from the Message.

"What marvellous love the Father has extended to us! Just look at it - we're called children of God! That's who we really are. But that's also why the world doesn't recognize us or take us seriously, because it has no idea who he is or what he's up to."

It's an extravagant, generous and marvellous love that he lavishes on us. Nothing is spared or held back. It's like going to a feast where there is almost too much to eat, you feel you want to try a bit of everything that is laid out but there's just too much. You don't want to miss anything but you don't have the capacity to try everything. The Father's love is like that, it's overwhelmingly extravagant and generous. Feel free to be greedy, there is more than enough to go round and it will never run out. Whatever you do or wherever you go, you will not be able to exhaust his love for us. When I was at school, at mealtimes there were twelve boys sat at a table, six on each side, with a teacher at the head. One particular teacher would cut the meal into fourteen portions which, after we were all served, left one portion for seconds. Of course, we all wanted seconds and so the teacher would cut this one piece into twelve bits so none of us were disappointed. Needless to say, each bit was not very substantial. Our Father is not like that, he doesn't have to ration his love or share it round, there is always enough.

At the start of this chapter I looked briefly at imperfect parental love and how that can limit what we expect from our Father. His love, however, is perfect. Sadly we don't know what perfect love is. How can we know what is perfect if we've never experienced it? I hope you all have had at least one person in your life who you know really loved you. When you were with them you felt special, you felt valued and were affirmed. Well, take that love and magnify it beyond your wildest dreams, that will start to give you an idea of what perfect love would be like. The ultimate in value, security, affirmation and acceptance. Our Father's love is perfect.

It is also a redemptive love. In order for us to be called his children he had to redeem us or buy us back from the enemy who'd stolen us. There was a price which had to be paid before we could be placed back in his family. Before we were children we were orphans (John 14:18). He took us from the destructive life of sin and brought us back into his family. Our Father's love is redemptive.

Have you ever thought how kind the Father is? He overlooks all our wrongdoings and failings. His love is unconditional and not a reward for the things we do right and then withheld when we do things wrong. It covers all the frustrations of life. Paul writes about us being clothed in love (Colossians 3:14), and so all the Father sees is the covering of love and not the mess which is being hidden underneath. In fact, what the Father sees is his son, Jesus, because we are hidden in Christ, we are kept safe in his love. Our Father's love is kind.

Our Father's love is also a giving love. He gives when we have needs, he gives when we don't have needs – he does it simply for the sake of giving and he even gives when we don't deserve it. Sometimes I think we have a very narrow view of giving. We want to receive financial gifts or practical things like food or clothing as we may be desperate for them in order to survive. However, they are not the only ways in which our Father gives to us. His gifts are all around us. The fact that you drove to work safely this morning, the beautiful countryside or parks near your home or work, the things you enjoy in your recreational time, good food or good times with friends. These can all be gifts we freely receive from our Father. Many years ago we used to sing a song, 'count your blessings name then one by one, count your blessings see what God has done'. Worry is a big thing for many people, but Jesus encourages us not worry but to trust our Father in Heaven (Matthew 6:25-34). He knows what we need and we are more important to him than the birds of the air or the flowers of the field. His blessings, of keeping it, hence the need to be constantly reminded. His promise has never changed nor has it ever lost any of its strength of meaning.

This covenant is also quoted in the New Testament but in a much more personal way.

"I will be a Father to you, and you shall be my sons and daughters." (2 Corinthians 6:18)

The love of the Father is extravagant. It is almost beyond comprehension and maybe that's a good thing. It's not meant to be understood or comprehended, it's meant to be experienced and lived in. It's no wonder that Jesus, in John 15, exhorts to remain, or live, in his love. Paul repeats this by encouraging us to be rooted and grounded in love and to be clothed in love. John, in his letters, writes about us living in love. Living in love is the outworking of being loved.

There is a place we may have to go before our heart is ready to receive the outpouring of his love and that is the wilderness (Jeremiah 31:2-3). The wilderness can be a lonely place where we feel deeply exposed and vulnerable. It may be an uncomfortable and frightening place, where the heat and pressure to survive are overwhelming. We may want to try and escape but this may be the very place where Father reveals himself to us in a tangible and powerful way. The wilderness was the place where many of the Old Testament saints had their significant encounters with God. There is a depth to an encounter with the Father when we meet him in vulnerability and weakness. A change takes place in our heart that we might not otherwise be able to experience. It is there we find his favour and grace. It is an encounter that gives rest and maybe for the first time, true contentment. Don't despise the wilderness. In fact, you may need to choose to go there in order to allow your heart to encounter love.

The love of the Father draws us into a relationship. It does not give us a lot of facts or information on how to live a good life. It's the relationship that changes us, not the religious enslavement to the law. Living loved will transform your life in a way you've never been able to experience before. Living loved will give you a security in your life that comes from the affirmation of Almighty God, who just happens to be your Father. Living loved will give you a peace that is supernatural.

To me, this is what Christianity is all about. Us living in the Father's love. We are placed in the eternal love of the Father because of his eternal covenant with us. Life flows from him, it is not the result of a choice we've made. We can only live in love because God is a Father to us. This is what he has always wanted, it's the only plan he's ever had, and he's done everything to make it happen.

What is 'it'?

As I conclude part one, let me draw these threads together so you can fully perceive the thing that will really change everything.

Chapter Five

The Most Excellent Way

I became a Christian when I was ten years old. It was the last evening of a youth camp and I responded to a very simple word given by the speaker. I can still remember it. His picture was someone standing on a railway bridge looking down along the tracks. Perspective makes it look as if the two tracks come together at some point in the distance. His gospel message was that it's easy to think, one day, our life will automatically merge with Jesus and we'll suddenly discover that we've been born again. Not true, he said. Like the railway tracks, our life will always run parallel and we therefore need to make a conscious decision to leave our track and step onto Jesus' one.

As a ten year old boy I responded and got off the track of my life and onto the track of Jesus. It was a very serious decision as I knew it was a decision which would affect the rest of my life.

To be honest it was nothing really to do with love. It was an acknowledgment that I needed my sins forgiven and the only way for that to happen was to come to Jesus, believe that he had taken my sin and I then had eternal life. It was the recognition that my life needed to change course and that Jesus had bridged the gap between me and God.

I don't remember how God was portrayed on that evening. I do know, however, that he was not portrayed as a loving Father. All I remember was there was a gap between me and him and that the only way to bridge that gap was through the gift of salvation, given to me through Jesus.

I am so glad I had that evening and even more glad that I responded. I've been on Jesus' track for nearly fifty years.

When people talk about us going back to our first love it's not something I understand, as I really don't think love featured highly on the evening I became a Christian. I know I'm in love with Jesus more now than I was when I was ten years old. It's the same with marriage, I'm more in love with Fiona now than I was when we first met. Love deepens and matures over time. We grow into a fulness of love. We become rooted and grounded in love. It's not where we start. I like what Henri Nouwen said about going back to our first love, "our first love is we love because he **first** loved us".

I would say it was many years after I'd become a Christian before love became a noticeable response of my heart. I truly believe that we can only love God once we have started to experience him loving us (1 John 4:19). He is loving us all the time, that is not in question, but our ability to receive love is something that grows and deepens over time.

For me, like many of you, I've lived in the blessing of one of the greatest gifts we can ever receive. The gift of salvation, our sins being forgiven and knowing that somehow we have been made right with God. Even knowing all that, we are still afraid of this God, we don't know him like we know Jesus. We don't experience him like we experience the Holy Spirit. Although he longs to be known, he is unknown by us. We're not quite sure of him. One of the lies that Satan placed in the heart of humanity was that God can't be trusted – "did God really say?" A question of doubt about our Father. There is a residue of that lie in each one of us and it can take years, even after we've become a Christian, for that lie to be washed fully away.

Don't get me wrong, salvation is a wonderful gift. We certainly didn't deserve it, we can't earn it or pay for it. It is a completely free gift based on the Father's love and mercy.

But this is where we can make a big mistake. We can allow this gift to become a hindrance to us, rather than it being the doorway into a life of freedom, a life like the one Jesus lived.

Our salvation is not an end in itself. It is not simply a ticket to Heaven and a guarantee of eternal life. Both of these are wonderful, almost too good to be true. But they are true, totally true.

We say we are born again. We are! We are born again in order to live as Jesus lived. We are born again in order that Christ may live in us. We are born again into a life of love.

"See what great love the Father has lavished on us, that we should be called children of God! And that is what we are! The reason the world does not know us is that it did not know him." (1 John 3:1)

Salvation is the step each one of us has to take in order that we become free to walk as Jesus walked (1 John 2:6). It is the key to us living a completely new life following on from our new birth. A birth is always the start of a new life. A baby is born and begins a journey lasting many decades. A baby doesn't remain a baby but grows up into the life it was born to live. It's the same for us. We are born again, but that is only the start of a new life.

This new life is to be a son or daughter to our Father. Sadly, this is often missed as we are side-tracked and led astray.

Before I look at how we've been side-tracked I want to look at the life of Jesus, the perfect son and our elder brother who showed us how to live in relationship with the Father.

After Jesus' birth the next encounter with him is as a twelve year old boy visiting the temple. He has gone with his parents to the festival in Jerusalem. The only trouble is that he doesn't go home with them. At the end of a day's travel from Jerusalem, Mary and Joseph realise that Jesus is not with them. They return to the city and spend three days looking for him, eventually finding him in the temple where he is talking to the leaders and the teachers. In fact, we read it is the teachers who are asking Jesus questions and he is answering them. Not only that but they are amazed at the answers he gives them. A twelve year old boy teaching the teachers! When Jesus is asked why he hadn't started the journey home with his parents his reply has a beautiful childlike simplicity about it.

"Why were you searching for me?" he asked. "Didn't you know I had to be in my Father's house?" But they did not understand what he was saying to them. (Luke 2:49-50)

Seemingly, Mary and Joseph did not understand what Jesus meant, so he submitted himself to them and returned home to Nazareth.

Even as twelve year old boy, Jesus only had one focus and that was to be in his Father's house doing his Father's business. For him, at that moment, it meant talking to the teachers, no doubt about his Father and his Kingdom. I can only imagine the awe and wonder that the teachers felt as this young lad brought revelation to their hearts and minds. I doubt they ever forgot that day.

We can give Jesus many titles: king of kings, teacher, miracle worker, healer, prophet, evangelist, friend. They're all true but for Jesus, none of them defined who he was. After his baptism he went into the wilderness where he was tempted by Satan. Each of the accusations started with "if you are the Son of God". Satan's attacks on Jesus were aimed at his identity, his relationship with his Father. Satan tried to undermine this relationship and failed. Jesus was so secure in who he was that he could rebuff Satan and walk away from the attack.

One day Jesus would heal someone, on another he would provide food, another time he would walk on water or go fishing. He was free to do all these things because he only did the things his Father gave him to do. He was not limited or constrained by a function or a particular type of ministry gifting. He was simply motivated by his relationship with his Father. He lived as a son to his Father, only concerning himself with his Father's will. Being a prophet, teacher or healer was irrelevant, they were not the motivating force behind his life. Being a son was.

When we look closely at the life of Jesus, we see that his identity was not defined by what he did but by who he was. He lived his whole life as a son and it did not matter if he was raising the dead, walking on water or feeding hungry people. It did not matter if he was teaching, prophesying or healing. He could move freely and seamlessly between different functions and not place a greater value on some over others. His function was not his identity. His identity was being a son to his Father. He did nothing for his own benefit or to make himself look good, everything he did was done to bring glory to his Father.

Before Paul continues his instructions concerning the life of the church he lays this foundation of love. The foundation of the Father's love is the only foundation on which the various gifts can be built. It is the only foundation which will bring life and prevent us from living in performance and being driven by activity and busyness. Without the foundation of love we will be a noisy gong, we won't have anything to give and nothing to gain (1 Corinthians 13:1-3). Whatever we do and whoever we are has to be based on the foundation of Father's love being constantly poured into our heart through the Holy Spirit. This is not just a better way, it is the most excellent way.

It is too easy to focus on our gifting or calling and to try to develop them into something beautiful and worthwhile. If we miss the foundation of love we will be building on sand rather than on solid rock.

The gifts are good but they are not the most excellent way.

I have laboured this for one very simple reason. The traditional pathway for most Christians is to be born again and then to have to try to find their place or function in the body of Christ. Somehow the foundation of love is bypassed and we journey into a life of ministry, calling and function. This is not the way Jesus lived. Yes, we see the gifts of the Spirit in action throughout his earthly life but we see them from the foundation of love. We see them as gifts rather than a ministry tool.

If we bypass the way of love and pursue a life of ministry or function, we are not walking as Jesus walked.

God, the Father, is the source of love. Our relationship with him is purely based on love. The issue is not God's ability to love us (that is constant), the issue is our ability to receive his love. The only way we can live as sons and daughters is for us to receive and live in his love, not as a one-off event but the constant flow of his love into our heart. We will discover the life of sonship as we become rooted and grounded in love. We discover that there is no limit to his love for us, we truly are being loved with an eternal love.

The last words Jesus said before being taken away to the cross are the fulfilment of everything he came to achieve for his Father. He wants us to know the Father and to know that we are loved in exactly the same way as he is loved. The way the Father loves the Son is exactly the same way that he loves us.

"I have made you known to them, and will continue to make you known, in order that the love you have for me may be in them and that I myself may be in them." (John 17:26)

"I have revealed to them who you are and I will continue to make you even more real to them, so that they may experience the same endless love that you have for me, for your love will now live in them, even as I live in them!" (John 17:26 TPT)

Jesus lived his whole life as a son. When we start to walk as Jesus walked, we too will live as sons and daughters to our Father. Salvation is a precious gift but it is not principally the doorway to a life of ministry and function. It is the doorway to sonship. First and foremost we are called to be sons and daughters, living in relationship with the Father just as Jesus did. This is eternal life (John 17:3).

Our problem is that we have not been led into a life of sonship. In being side-tracked into what is good and certainly desirable, we have missed the very best. The most excellent way of love. At the end of 1 Corinthians 13 and the start of chapter 14 Paul tells us that love (the Father's love for us) is the greatest gift and then encourages us to pursue love, or make it our greatest aim.

When we see that the purpose of our salvation is to live as sons and daughters, it will change everything.

Chapter Six

"What Must I Do?"

We have been tricked. Like any trick, or trap, it had to look attractive in order that we might fall for it. The trap I'm talking about took place in a garden and it was easy to fall into it because it looked so attractive.

It began with a lie. "If you eat from the tree of knowledge of good and evil then you will become like God". For Adam and his wife that must have been a very attractive proposition. It's often the yearning of our hearts as well; we want to be like God, and we'll do anything to try and make it happen. The problem is that this motivation to 'do' something is completely the wrong one. We can't do anything to become like God. This trick, although a lie, was actually based on a truth. Adam and his wife were already like God as they'd been created in his image or in his likeness. They couldn't achieve it through their own performance.

Our true identity has always been that we are sons and daughters, and this is not something we achieve through performance, it is a gift simply because God is our Father. Satan tricked mankind into believing that they would enter their true identity by being motivated to do the right thing or by trying hard not to do the wrong thing. A performance of trying to discern what is good and then seeking to do it, and, likewise, deciding what is evil and steering well away from it.

Satan's trick was to present the tree of knowledge of good and evil as a good thing, the blueprint of how to live a life that pleased God. He made it look like the route to becoming like God, knowing good from evil. It sounded so good. Sadly, though it was not the way to life but the way to death, the destruction of our relationship with our Father.

For us to determine what is right or wrong leads to us making judgments or assessments which we can only do from the fallen perspective of humanity. God, however, can judge between good and evil, right and wrong, from the eternal perspective of being the perfect, loving Father. His judgment is flawless and complete whereas ours is imperfect and incomplete.

Unfortunately, the trick worked and mankind thought it knew better than God. The outworking of that fatal mistake has been centuries of conflict, division and independence. One man's right is another man's wrong.

But the lie has a deeper deception. Wanting to be like God leads to us trying to work out how we can best please him. What do I have to do to make God pleased with me? How can I make God notice me? What the tree of knowledge of good and evil has done is to corrupt our thinking. We recognise we have a problem and so we try to resolve it on our own. This is very different to the gospel which recognises we have a problem and that there is nothing we can do to fix it. We need a Saviour and we are given one in Jesus.

Traditionally, when we think of this tree in the garden we think about the implications of evil and what is wrong or bad. When we realise it is the tree of knowledge of good **as much** as it is the knowledge of evil our whole perspective or thinking changes. Trying to do the right thing has the same root as trying not to do the wrong thing. Trying to be good has the same root as trying not to be bad.

It becomes focussed on our own effort. It becomes all about us trying to become righteous through our works, that's self-righteousness.

Whenever something is based on our effort, we become the centre. The focus is then on what we can achieve or accomplish and we are subtly pulled away from living as sons and daughters and drawn into a servant hearted way of life. In short, we lose our sonship and end up becoming servants.

I hope you can see the deepening consequences of the original trap in the garden. We are led to believe that we can be like God (knowing good and evil). We form our imperfect and incomplete judgments which lead to a works-based life rather than one flowing out of love. We end up trying to please God through our actions rather than resting in his pleasure of us, simply because he is our Father and we are his children. We become driven by the law, which becomes the standard by which we measure ourselves.

The trap is very effective at drawing us away from our eternal identity as sons and daughters. Our Father loves us with an eternal love and he has a permanent place for each one of us in his family. We are no longer slaves or servants but children of God (Galatians 4:6-7). We have no need to fulfil all the requirements of the law in order to make ourselves right with God. All those requirements were fulfilled on our behalf by Jesus. He did not abolish the law but he did what was impossible for us to do. And by doing so he has set us free from the law of sin and death and from an obligation to the law of Moses. He has set us free to live by the law of the Spirit of life in Christ Jesus (Romans 7:21-8:2). He has set us free from climbing the wrong tree and has brought us back to the Father's original plan; to be recipients of his grace and mercy. We are free from a servant hearted way of life.

It's interesting that this tree is called the tree of 'knowledge' of good and evil. It's not the experience of good and evil but rather the knowledge of it. How different to the tree of life which is not knowledge of life but the experience of life itself.

This, my friends, is how we have lived. We have been barking up the wrong tree.

We have been led down the wrong path, tricked into thinking that doing the right thing is good and that it will make us like God. Of course, there is a lot of value in doing good things. Society works best when people obey the rules which have been put in place to make it work.

For example, it is definitely a good thing, in the UK, to drive on the left hand side of the road. We don't have to think about it, we do it automatically. Hopefully, it's automatic to stop at a red light, as not to do so would probably cause an accident. In society there are consequences for us if we choose to do the wrong thing.

We do not relate to God in the same way as we follow the rules set by society. Relating to God, as we have seen, is a heart relationship, it is the experience of being loved and of living loved. It is the experience of life.

The secret is not to climb the tree of knowledge of good and of evil, remember that is a trick. It's a trick we don't have to have fall for. The secret is to feed from the tree of life.

This picture that I've painted is probably all too familiar for many of us. There is a busyness and weariness that comes from seeking to do the right thing in order to please God or find favour with him. We plough our own furrow rather than taking his yoke and walking in union with him. There is an unconscious belief that many of us have: "We are saved by grace and not through our own works, but then we have to work hard in order to maintain or keep our salvation". You will not hear that belief being openly expressed but you will see it being worked out in people's lives. In fact, don't look at how it may work out in other people, look at how it manifests itself in your own life. We should never point the finger at others but rather keep the focus on our own heart.

In the story of Gideon (Judges 7), his resources are reduced to such an extent that it is impossible for him to achieve anything in his own strength or through his strategic planning. He has to rely on Israel's salvation being a gift from God. Three hundred men was impossible odds, but they are the very sort of odds that God likes working with. The impossibility of man's situation becomes the channel through which God acts.

The rich young ruler came to Jesus (Mark 10) with a simple, yet wrong, question – 'What must I do?". Jesus takes him through all the right things he needs to do but the young man, having done them all his life, is not satisfied. What more can there be to do when you've feel you've already done everything?

The trap that we so often fall for wants us to believe that our relationship with God is all about what we have to do (or not do). It's a trick and it does not lead to life. In fact, as it comes from the enemy, it will never lead to life but always to something being stolen from us and, therefore, something inside of us dying. The tree of knowledge of good and of evil is basically a self-destruct button which we are pretty good at pressing.

Christianity as we have known it, has been about pursuing knowledge of right and wrong and then trying hard to stay the right side of the line in order to please God. The pursuit of knowledge will lead us into misguided action or works.

what he gives us and what he has made easy by preparing in advance for us.

For us to understand this we need to see with the eyes of our heart. A consequence of Adam and his wife eating from the wrong tree was that their eyes were opened (Genesis 3:7). Clearly this is not referring to their natural eyes and must therefore mean another set of eyes. As this is in the context of knowledge, it must be the eyes of their mind that were opened and the age of reason began. When we give priority to the eyes of our mind, the eyes of our heart become dull and cease to see things as they really are. It is for this reason that Paul prays that the eyes of our heart may be opened (or enlightened). He reverses what began in the garden and leads us back to seeing God for who he really is and therefore enabling us to believe who we really are; sons and daughters of a loving Father (Ephesians 1:17-18)

What you have read may be a challenge. Like the rich young ruler, you may be accustomed to asking "what must I do?" You may feel you've spent your life doing all the right things. You may believe it is right to do things for God. You may want to work for him and see his will accomplished on the earth. You may wonder what on earth I am talking about. You may disagree with me. Let me state clearly, I do believe in doing things for God. The question I am posing is much more to do with our motivation or heart attitude, rather than our specific actions. Are you motivated by the tree of life or by the tree of knowledge of good and of evil? Remember the consequences of that tree; we want to be like God so we

87

form imperfect judgments which lead us into a works based lifestyle rather than being rooted and grounded in love.

When we realise that we are principally recipients rather than doers it changes everything. It's a seismic change and one only brought about through the revelation and experience of being loved by the Father. Many people often tell me they've had their life turned upside down by the Father's love. Actually, what happens is our life is turned the right way up. Instead of walking on our hands we start to walk on our feet and wonder why it is so much easier. We start to live as we were meant to live. We were born to be receivers, recipients of the downward flow of life from Heaven. Anything else is a trick or a trap and I encourage you not to fall for it. Let everything change as you begin to live in the river of Father's love flowing into your heart.

It will change everything.

Chapter Seven

Our Obedience

Between the age of twelve and eighteen I went to a boarding school. I soon discovered that, for school life to run "smoothly", there were a whole series of rules which had to be obeyed. There were seven houses at school and about thirty boys lived in each house. Each house was presided over by a housemaster and his wife, the housemistress. My house was Clyde, our house colour was green and my number was CL17. The morning routine is still indelibly printed on my memory and I could easily recite it for you. My house parents were godly people, who, despite having no children of their own, had a heart for all of us. They had spent many years in Ghana as missionaries, working at a Christian School. My housemaster also had a military background and was the Captain of the school's cadet force.

Each morning, wake up time was 6.55am and shortly before the appointed hour one of the junior boys (who had the house alarm clock by his bed) would wake up and then on the dot of 6.55 would run round the dormitories shouting loudly, "five to seven, time to get up". The first time this duty fell to me I was too timid and did not shout loudly enough and everybody was late down. You can guess who got the blame for that. In order to keep the school fees down there were no cleaners and the first job of the day was for us boys to do house cleaning. Bare wooden floors were polished by hand,

89

sinks and toilets cleaned and brass door handles polished.

All of these jobs were supervised by a prefect (one of the older boys). Failure to do anything to the required standard led to an automatic, non-questionable punishment handed out by the prefect. In the last two years of my time at school I, too, was a prefect and had my chance of being able to hand out the "extra work" punishments. Recently, one of the guys in the year below me posted a picture of the 'extra work' book on Facebook. The page he'd chosen was all in my handwriting; I'd punished boys for talking too loudly, not cleaning shoes properly or being disrespectful at mealtimes. Such power!

Rules were not to be questioned, only obeyed. Many of them seemed pointless and, whilst we questioned them amongst ourselves, we would never dare do it publicly. I was at school at the start of the punk rock era and the advent of boys having their ears pierced. One very brave boy came back after the holidays with his ear pierced and when the headmaster saw it, he pulled it out. I think that hurt, but probably not as much as the corporal punishment that followed.

Of the seven houses, mine, probably, had the reputation of being the strictest. Therefore rules had to be obeyed and obeyed all the time.

We only had lessons on two afternoons each week with the others being given over to scouts or cadets, clubs and societies and two dreaded (by me) sports afternoons. Nothing in me wanted to be in the army cadets so I joined the scouts, eventually gaining the Chief Scouts Award. Every Monday afternoon we were doing useful things like learning how to tie knots, whilst the cadets were being marched round the school grounds. Anyone who has been in the cadets, like the military, will know that there is only one point of an order and that is for it to be obeyed.

On one occasion I was in the cricket nets letting a friend of mine practice his bowling. I took a very fast (and hard) cricket ball on an ungloved thumb which spilt open with blood pouring everywhere. We were next to the school medical centre so we went across the road and the school nurse bandaged it up for me. On returning to my house I was summoned by the housemistress and told off for going to the medical centre without first having obtained her permission. It would have been a ten minute walk back to the house, find the housemistress, obtain the required permission and then a ten minute walk back to the medical centre. All the while with the top of my thumb hanging off. That was one rule I never understood.

Towards the end of my time at school I started having driving lessons. We had some old cars that we could drive around the school site without going onto any public roads. The school was on a large country estate so there was plenty of space to drive around without supervision. It was great fun. Of course, when you learn to drive there are two parts: one is the actual driving and the other the Highway Code, the rules of the road. These are the rules to keep you and other road users safe and, as many of us know, there are penalties for failing to keep these rules.

One final school story which maybe shows how grace can be applied when the rules have been broken: In my last year we had a new headmaster and one of the first changes he made was to allow us to go out to the pub, but only when we were eighteen years old. One of the guys in our group of friends had been put up a year and so he was only seventeen when the rest of us were eighteen. On his 17th birthday we couldn't very well go and celebrate his birthday without him so we hid away and had the party on site. We were caught! The next day we were all before the headmaster who told us the normal punishment would be for us to be expelled. Thankfully, he showed mercy and let us off with a verbal warning and a letter to our parents.

After leaving school I trained to be an accountant and have been doing that for the last forty years. I shan't bore you with too much detail but will just mention the series of manuals one of my colleagues has on his shelf. Twenty ring binders, each one twelve centimetres thick which contain all the UK tax law. The rules by which my profession must abide. Clearly the tax authorities like it when people follow the rules, and yes, you've guessed it, there are a series of penalties for failure to do so.

Schools have rules but so do workplaces, families, churches and of course society. Rules are there for a purpose and, particularly in society, keeping them should allow for harmonious living. In families there are rules but hopefully they are laid on a foundation of love and relationship which ultimately supersede and go beyond the rules. In a family the rules are often overridden for the greater good of relationship and unity. A family which insists on compliance with the rule book will not be a happy family. A friend of mine, wisely, once said "knowing when to break the rules can be as important as knowing when to keep them".

In our thinking, obeying rules and regulations has become associated with authority which in turn is associated with control. We see this in our schools with the teacher/pupil relationship; it's there in our work places between the boss and the staff and we see it in society between the civil authorities and us, the people. One place we shouldn't see it is in the church. The control which often runs alongside the requirement for obedience can, if we're not careful, take away our uniqueness as we are squashed into the mould of conformity.

We have a life fashioned by rules and regulations and, therefore, our understanding of obedience has become a behavioural issue rather than a heart one. Sadly, it is also the way we view our behaviour towards God. Is this how it was meant to be?

Before we go much further we need to understand the relational nature of the ten commandments. Old Testament Hebrew culture understood something we fail to grasp. They knew that every command given by God had a relational foundation as they were an expression of his heart and his love for his people. Remember God is love and therefore everything he does is from love, done with love and done for love. The ten commandments are an indication of what our lives will look like if we desire to be like him. Instead of reading them as a command we should read them like this:

"There is nothing in me that would ever steal, murder or destroy relationships, if you want to be like me why would you ever want to steal, murder or commit adultery."

We read them as a command, something to be obeyed whereas they were given as an expression of the nature and character of our Heavenly Father. They show us what he is like and the more we live in love the more we will want to do what they say. Following the ten commandments was always meant to be primarily a relational, heart response and not a behavioural one.

Just before Moses received the ten commandments, God reminds the people of their past and how he has been faithful to them in bringing them out of Egypt. He reiterates his covenant with them and shows them the fruitful consequences of walking in his ways.

"Then Moses went up to God, and the Lord called to him from the mountain and said, "This is what you are to say to the descendants of Jacob and what you are to tell the people of Israel: 'You yourselves have seen what I did to

Egypt, and how I carried you on eagles' wings and brought you to myself. Now if you obey me fully and keep my covenant, then out of all nations you will be my treasured possession. Although the whole earth is mine, you will be for me a kingdom of priests and a holy nation.' These are the words you are to speak to the Israelites." (Exodus 19:3-6)

These are not words of condemnation or judgement. They are words of hope and the promise of a good future.

Having received the ten commandments, Moses returns to the people only to find that they've made a golden calf. In his anger he smashes the stone tablets and goes on to destroy the golden idol the people had made. God does not reject his people because of their rebellion, instead he gives them a second chance. Moses goes back up the mountain to receive the commandments once again. Before he starts out he has a powerful, yet intimate, encounter with God.

"Moses said to the Lord, "You have been telling me, 'Lead these people,' but you have not let me know whom you will send with me. You have said, 'I know you by name and you have found favour with me.' If you are pleased with me, teach me your ways so I may know you and continue to find favour with you. Remember that this nation is your people." The Lord replied, "My Presence will go with you, and I will give you rest." Then Moses said to him, "If your Presence does not go with us, do not send us up from here." (Exodus 33:12-15)

In these few short verses, Moses goes from wanting to know how to get a job done (*who is coming with me, teach me your ways*) to earnestly desiring God's presence.

It is in that place of being totally immersed in God's presence that Moses embarks on his journey up the mountain. It is here that he has a profound revelation of the nature and personality of God. He now understands what God is really like as he has seen and experienced his presence. (We will look more closely at this journey in the next chapter.)

"And he passed in front of Moses, proclaiming, "The Lord, the Lord, the compassionate and gracious God, slow to anger, abounding in love and faithfulness, maintaining love to thousands, and forgiving wickedness, rebellion and sin. Yet he does not leave the guilty unpunished; he punishes the children and their children for the sin of the parents to the third and fourth generation." (Exodus 34:6-7)

As we read the narrative of Israel's history we see a God who does not judge or condemn but who always give a second chance. We see a God who is more concerned with his people enjoying his presence rather than following the rule book. We see the nature of God being expressed: compassionate, gracious, loving, slow to anger, full of lovingkindness and forgiving. We do not see an angry, distant God, we see a loving Father. We discover what our Father is really like.

We have to see everything that God has said in the context of relationship. As we do it will begin to change everything.

It is absolutely right to say that the Bible talks a lot about obedience. Jesus talks about obedience and so it is not something that miraculously disappears once we start reading the New Testament. I don't believe that obedience is the issue. What matters is our heart. As I have said, obedience to God's word is a relational response rather than a behavioural one.

Something did change between the first covenant and the second one. In the first covenant, obedience came to mean compliance with the law and therefore submission to the authorities who sought to impose it. It meant fear of punishment or judgement for failing to keep the law. Obedience became tied to rules and regulations in a way it was never meant to be. Obedience was no longer a relational response but a legalistic one. It became oppressive rather than liberating.

And that is where many of us are today. We have become stuck in a rules based religion rather than living in the glorious freedom of the sons of God.

When Jesus was asked about obedience to the law he made it very simple. He went right back to the relational foundation of love and summed it up in a few words:

"Love the Lord you God with all your heart, soul and mind and love your neighbour as yourself."

Our relationship with God started with love. All God has ever wanted is to be a Father to us. Jesus sums up the law by restating the main thing, love.

A subtle, yet powerful change has taken place in our thinking. The law demands obedience and so, if we live by the law, we will be constantly seeking to do the right thing. Obedience has become the way through we which we try and find God's pleasure and approval. This is a fear based way of living, motivated by a system of reward or punishment. Fear, however, is not compatible with love. Love perfects (or makes us complete) whereas fear condemns us (1 John 4:17-18)

Something in us needs to change if we are to move away from a dogmatic, subservience to rules and regulations. If you are like the rich young ruler and believe you are doing all the right things but are not finding life, then I have some good news for you. It doesn't have to be this way.

The old covenant focuses on our obedience being the way to fulfil the law, whereas the new covenant desires a relationship. When we live under the old covenant, obedience becomes the goal of our life and in so doing it has swapped places with love.

Paul encourages us to pursue love, or to make it our greatest aim (1 Corinthians 14:1). Love is the goal of our Christian life, not obedience.

In John 14 Jesus says the same thing in three slightly different ways.

"Loving me empowers you to obey my commands." (v15 TPT)

"Those who truly love me are those who obey my commands. Whoever passionately loves me will be passionately loved by my Father." (v21 TPT)

"Jesus replied, 'Anyone who loves me will obey my teaching.'" (v23)

Obedience flows from love. It is not the other way round.

All too often what we believe, or what we put on ourselves and on other people, is: "if we obey God enough, then he will start to love us". Whilst we may never say those words it is the underlying belief that fashions much of thinking and behaviour. It therefore determines the nature of our relationship with God. We are still seeking to live under the old covenant of obedience to the law (behaviour), believing it is the way to gain God's approval and acceptance. There is nothing we can do to obtain God's approval, we already have it. We are accepted and loved simply because he is our Father and we are his children. Approval and acceptance are not derived from actions or behaviour but flow from relationship. We are the beloved.

Obedience is relational, not behavioural.

In fact, when you love someone obedience ceases to be obedience and instead becomes a desire to please. You seek out the other person's longings and it is your love for them which motivates you to do the things that please them. This is what Jesus is talking about in John 14. Love produces obedience. This is the very thing King David prophesied in Psalm 40.

Sacrifice and offering you did not desire
but my ears you have opened;
burnt offerings and sin offerings you did not require.
Then I said, "Here I am, I have come;
it is written about me in the scroll.
I desire to do your will, my God;
your law is within my heart. (Psalm 40:6-8)

Obedience is based on rules, desire is based on relationship.

Very often obedience is a choice we make. We make an assessment and choose one thing over another. That choice can easily happen in our mind. It can be a rational or logical approach leading to what we believe is the right course of action. Our heart may not necessarily be involved in the process at all. You will recognise this as living from the wrong tree that I talked about in the previous chapter.

Yet the obedience Jesus talks about is rooted in the heart. It is a heart decision based on love.

When we know that we are loved, we will be able to respond with love. Our response of love is always dependent on us having first received his love. If we are not living in love we cannot respond with love and therefore we default to responding with greater compliance and more of the right behaviour. The obedience Jesus models is always the response of his love for his Father. He did not do anything because he had to, he did it because he wanted to.

What about us?

Does obedience mean compliance with a set of rules and regulations? Is there fear of punishment or condemnation? Do we do what we do because we feel we have to? Are we driven by right behaviour? These are questions for our heart.

If you answer those questions knowing that your obedience is a duty and obligation, then you are living under the old covenant.

We cannot manufacture the desire I've been talking about. It can only be the response to living in the Father's love. Our desire for him will grow the more our ability to receive his love increases.

When our heart is saturated with Father's love we will make an amazing discovery. It will be one that sets us free. Obedience will stop being duty and obligation; it will not be connected to rules and regulations; it will not be driven by fear. Obedience will cease to be obedience and will become a way of life where we seek and desire to do our Father's will. We will begin to walk as Jesus walked.

As we live in love we begin to see what is in the Father's heart. We see his desires and longings and everything in us will want to pursue them with all of our heart. When we have seen his heart, why wouldn't we want to walk in his ways.

Seeing this with the eyes of our heart will change everything.

Chapter 8

Living in Love

The underlying theme of this book is to pursue the longing in our heart for change. We have taken upon ourselves a yoke that has been heavy and often ended up being too hard to bear. The only way we can let go of this heavy yoke is to enter the fulness of the Father's love. As the Father is revealed to us we find the pathway of rest where our inner man can be stilled and be at peace (Matthew 11:25-30).

Sometimes I think we read the Bible and see a glimpse of what our lives could be like. We catch sight of God's glory and wonder how it might affect us. Often, we conclude that this is what it will be like when we eventually arrive in Heaven. It is too much for us to believe that what we have seen is for here and now. It seems to be beyond us and impossible to attain.

I want to tell you that it is possible to live in love. The Bible after all, is not given to guide us through Heaven, it is given to lead us each and every day that we live on planet earth. Everything contained in the Bible must therefore be possible for us achieve. It may be hard, there undoubtedly will be struggles and often things won't go according to our neat plans. Nonetheless, it is possible.

I imagine that many of you are beginning to feel as if you are not living in love. Maybe you make the occasional visit into love rather than knowing you've made your home there. I understand that. That's how I lived for many years. I can't give you a time and date when it changed, but now I know I live in love and, yes, although I take the occasional walk away from love, I know where my home is. Of course, the Father is loving us all the time but our background and circumstances prevent us from experiencing his love for us.

As I say, I can't give you a time and date when it changed. It's the journey of transformation that brings our heart home and then we know that we are living in Father's love. Too many people fear his judgement and that fear prevents them from choosing to pursue him and his love. Fear is always connected to punishment and it will hold us in prison. Love releases and drives out our fear, and that includes any fear of God's judgement.

I want to take you on a journey that Moses made which, I believe, has three separate phases. Moses made this journey in a few short verses, whereas, when we look at our lives, it often seems to be a journey of many months or even years. That's ok, the important thing is to be on the journey as it has a good destination as we shall see.

"Moses said to the Lord, "You have been telling me, 'Lead these people,' but you have not let me know whom you will send with me. You have said, 'I know you by name and you have found favour with me.' If you are pleased with me, teach me your ways so I may know you and

continue to find favour with you. Remember that this nation is your people." The Lord replied, "My Presence will go with you, and I will give you rest." Then Moses said to him, "If your Presence does not go with us, do not send us up from here. How will anyone know that you are pleased with me and with your people unless you go with us? What else will distinguish me and your people from all the other people on the face of the earth?" (Exodus 33:12-15)

Moses is panicking! He is faced with the almost impossible job of leading the Israelite nation across the desert and into the promised land. Can you imagine all the strategic planning and leadership which would have been necessary. All the people skills needed to lead a people who had never made such a journey before. All the military plans in case they were attacked whilst on their journey. It was huge job and one not made any easier by the constant rebellion of the people. Certainly not an easy task.

Moses' first response is, "Help, I can't do this on my own! Who is going to help me?" A cry of human despair and one we often find ourselves crying out. "Help, I can't do this!" The task in front of us, the necessary transformation of our heart, seems too big for us to contemplate, let alone accomplish. Maybe this needs to be the first step; a recognition that we can't make this journey on our own. We need help.

Having faced the enormity of the task and his own weakness, Moses remembers that God has appointed him to this position of leadership. He has found favour in God's eyes. That should have been comforting but it was not enough. Moses needed something more. Realising he can't do it on his own pushes Moses into the second phase of the journey. He asks God to show him his ways, in other words he wants to be told what to do. In effect, he is asking for the instruction manual – "what do I have to do in order to accomplish this impossible task?"

Like Moses, once we realise that we don't have the resources to change ourselves, we cry out for the rule book: "what should I be doing?" It's a natural response and a place where many of us sadly remain, often for many years. In fact, we can remain in that place until the groaning in our heart propels us out of, "what must I do?" and into the next and most significant phase of the journey.

Moses could have done the job if he had followed the instructions contained in the 'how to' manual; he could have obeyed the rules and been a successful leader. But it was not enough. This was not the end of Moses' journey and neither should be it be the end of ours. It is possible to enjoy and live in God's blessings by knowing his ways and seeking to obey them. God is so generous that that he will always bless our own efforts but it will always be limited to our own efforts. Doing the right thing will lead to a blessed life but it will not be the fully blessed life that we have been promised and that is our inheritance.

In the third and final phase of Moses' journey he realises that there is something greater than purely following God's ways. He hears the Father whisper, "My presence will go with you and I will give you rest". What a relief! The recognition of this is almost overwhelming for Moses as his response is, "your presence, if it's not with us, then we aren't going anywhere."

This is why I believe it's possible for us to live in love. If Moses could experience the presence of God then so can we. He saw that the only way to live life to the full was to be enveloped in the Father's love. My experience is that too many people are happy to remain at the second stage of the journey, being content with following the instruction manual. They therefore miss out on the intimacy and security of entering into God's presence where we are surrounded by love. I encourage you to continue and discover the joy and intimacy of centring yourself in his love and his presence.

Moses made this journey in a few short verses. I hope by presenting his journey in this way, you will hasten through the first two stages into the resting place of his love. We too, like Moses, can say, "without your presence we're not moving". It's the recognition that our own strength, or the falsely perceived fruitfulness of doing the right thing, is not enough. There is the final phase of our journey which is to enter the Father's heart and to live life from the fulness of his presence.

The journey Moses made is also our journey. It is the realisation that the place of true contentment is within our grasp. The life Moses lived and the one Jesus promised is for us. The prize of moving from the stagnant, 'what must I do' stage, into the life-giving one, is rest for our souls (Matthew 11:29). This is what our heart desires, but sadly we don't often find it.

As we all know, there are times when it's nothing like the seemingly smooth (and quick) journey that Moses made. We become bogged down in the challenges of life or the woundedness of our heart. It feels as if our heart is engaged in an uphill struggle; two steps forward, one and half backward.

Jeremiah knew what this was like.

I don't know if you've ever read all of the book of Lamentations. It's not the most cheery book, but actually it is the story of our daily lives. We tend to only know a few verses from the middle of chapter three. However, if you read the whole chapter you will discover that the writer is having a bad day, or perhaps it may be a bad month or even year. He is overwhelmed by life and can't see his way ahead. His low point is in verse 18 when he says, *"so I say, my endurance has perished, so has my hope from the Lord"*. It's all become too much for Jeremiah.

It is precisely at this low point that he remembers something and it is this memory which probably saves him.

He remembers the Father's love. This great, saving, redeeming love revitalises his hope and gives him back his perspective on life. All was not lost, God is still faithful and loving. This is the redeeming factor: there is always hope because God is always good. His steadfast love never changes, never runs out and is always there for us.

When the going is tough, we too, can remember the faithful love of the Father. Although we may feel the opposite, his mercies will be new every morning. We can wait quietly for his salvation, even in the midst of our struggles. Great is his faithfulness!

This is not necessarily our automatic response. However, we can choose to point our heart towards his presence where there is rest and peace. We can point ourselves away from the storms of life and towards the safety of the harbour of his love. His love is strong enough to buffer all the things that life throws at us. As we wrap ourselves in his love our heart will grow stronger. We realise that we are not on our own. Our hearts are vulnerable, but when wrapped in his love they become protected and held in a safe place.

In John's first letter we read that we can "know and rely on the love God has for us, for God is love" (1 John 4:16). These are not words that find a home in our mind, they live in our heart as they are experiential words. They are words that describe a relationship and words that are proven to be true time and time again as we rest in Father's love. We know our Father is reliable and that distances us from us our own self-reliance. We find, as

Jesus said, that we are abiding in him (John 15) and that "the resting place of his love has become the very source and root of our life" (Ephesians 3:17 TPT).

Often, when we think about what living in love means, we believe it to be our love for other people; "How can I become a more loving person?" First and foremost though, we need to see that living in love is living in the Father's love. It is allowing him to make his home in our heart and discovering that our home is firmly rooted in the centre of his heart. It is a distraction for us to concentrate on our love for others; it's important, and I'll come onto it shortly, but it is not the central thing we should consider as we look at what living in love really means.

At the end of John 17 we see what living in love really is. Jesus shows us the longing of his heart: that we would be with him where he is (v24). As he only said the words he heard his Father saying, we can therefore assume that this is the Father's desire as well. Jesus is at his Father's side, in the centre of his presence and that, too, is the place where we can make our home. This is not the reward for good behaviour but is the freedom of relationship with our Heavenly Father. It is the inheritance that is ours as we live in Christ.

Living in love is within our grasp, it is attainable. We can live in the experience of being loved by our Father. Paul describes it as being rooted and grounded in love. Interestingly, he recognises that our heart is not strong enough to contain all the love the Father has for us. Our heart needs to be strengthened in order that it can expand to contain the fulness of the Father's love. I believe, as we are rooted and grounded in love, we receive the spirit of sonship which will set us free to walk as Jesus walked. It completely transforms us.

Living in love is the key to fear being driven from your heart. Fear is one of the biggest and most powerful forces which is trying to take control of your heart. It is the cause of many of your struggles and one of the biggest chains holding you captive. The perfect love of the Father will drive fear away. Making your home in love is the best and only antidote to fear. It's also a lot less stressful! It truly is our salvation.

This way, love has the run of the house, becomes at home and mature in us, so that we're free of worry on Judgment Day - our standing in the world is identical with Christ's. There is no room in love for fear. Well-formed love banishes fear. Since fear is crippling, a fearful life - fear of death, fear of judgment -is one not yet fully formed in love. (1 John 4:17-18 The Message)

To me, this is more than a revelation. A revelation is something we see that has previously been hidden. Yes, we need a revelation of the Father's love for us, but we need more. We need an impartation of his love into our heart. We need the substance of his love to be poured into our heart by and through the Holy Spirit (Romans 5:5).

I invite you to pause for a moment. Will you consider the journey Moses took and ask yourself which stage you are at. If you feel you are stuck in trying to do the right thing can I encourage you to seek his presence. Doing the right thing is not bad, it is just not the complete picture. Seeking his presence takes you further into the daily experience of living in love. The rich young ruler was also stuck with this question: "what must I do?" He was unable to move beyond it and so he went away sad and unfulfilled. Moving beyond this seemingly innocuous question is the doorway to life. It is the doorway into his presence which will enable you to experience the same profound relief as Moses.

It will change everything.

****

Before closing this chapter, I want to talk briefly about how this affects our love for one another. John says that as we love one another, God lives in us and his love is perfected (or made complete) in us (1 John 4:12). This does not mean that God's love for us is conditional on us loving other people. God's love is never conditional; it is always freely given and not dependent on anything we do or don't do. We don't seek love in order to give it away; we seek love purely for the sake of being loved. The fulfilment (or completion) of us being loved by the Father is the natural and automatic overflow of that love to others.

In the Old Testament there is an emphasis on the tribes of Israel which are centred around families. Family is also the theme running through the New Testament. Not the traditional nuclear family but the new family, with God as Father and us as his sons and daughters, living together as brothers and sisters. It is a family that loves and cares for one another.

Too often, I think, we have tried to create this family before we have come to know the Father. We have made loving one another our goal, hoping it would be natural and maybe even easy, only to discover the opposite. It has not been natural and certainly not been easy. We struggle to become the family we read about. I believe the reason for this is that we have tried to do things in the wrong order. We have majored on our love for other people, rather than on the Father's love for us. Living in love has, therefore, become people centred, rather than Father centred. We can only love because he first loved us. Living loved will lead to the immergence of family and this is the perfection (or completeness) of his love amongst us.

We need to rethink what we mean by living in love. It is not primarily our love for others but the Father's love for us. From this everything else flows, and as it does we will begin to treat others as the Father treats us. We will honour rather than judge. We will care rather than being indifferent and we will value others rather than competing against them. We will appreciate their contribution and want to see them praised rather than promoting ourselves.

As we live in love the relationships in our families, churches, workplaces and communities will change. Love will become the hallmark of our relationships.

Living in love will change everything.

****

In talking about the way we love one another I have chosen to highlight only one of the fruits of living in love. I believe every aspect of our church life will change as together we live in Father's love. Our worship will change, after all Jesus said 'true' worshippers will worship the Father in the Spirit and in truth. Our giving of both time and money will change; we have no need to worry about what we will eat or drink, we have a Father who will provide for us. As his children we can afford to be generous. Our theology (and therefore our teaching) will change as we become Father centred rather than seeking to control an activity based programme. Our children's and youth work will change; no longer will want to raise up servant-leaders, instead we will want to see sons and daughters walking in their glorious freedom and becoming like Jesus.

In short, every area of church life will change as a result of us being rooted and grounded in love.

Every area of our church life will change because every area of our personal life changes as we discover the enormity of what it means to live loved. The extent to which these things change is dependent on us ceasing to be motivated by "what must I do?" and desiring to be totally immersed in Father's love.

Here I add a final caution. Never take it upon yourself to try and change your church or its leaders. It doesn't work that way. A church is a community of people and the only way it can change is if individual people change. As we, individually, have our heart transformed and become rooted and grounded in love, so together our church family life will change. You can't change your church or its pastor, you can't change your family or friends. All you can do is let the hunger in your heart take you deeper into the reservoir of Father's love for you. This will be the magnet which attracts others into the journey of love.

Living in love will change everything, first and foremost it will change you.

Pause and Reflect

Before you read the final two chapters of this book I would like you to pause and reflect. This book is about change and so I trust you can recognise the hunger in your heart which has led you to this point in time. The frustration with the way things have been and the longing for something to be different.

As we have seen, the desire of Jesus' heart is that we should be with him where he is. He wants us to know that we are loved by the Father in exactly the same way as he is loved. This desire also becomes a seed in your heart, which is growing and prompting you to seek something greater than you've already experienced.

Something has been stolen from us and we've not been fully aware of the loss. We have lost intimacy and relationship with the Father and consequently have been dragged into living as servants or orphans. Spiritual death instead of life in all its fulness. We have lost sight of who our Father is and who we are.

In the Lion King, the cheeky monkey, Rafiki, leads Simba out into the wilderness where, in a vision, he encounters his father, Mufasa. In this vision Mufasa speaks to Simba and reminds him of his true identity.

"You have forgotten who you are and so have forgotten me. You are more than what you've become. Remember who you are, you are my son."

117

We too have lost sight of who we really are. We have forgotten our Father and so become much less than we were meant to be. We need to hear our Father speaking those same words over us and be reminded once again of who we really are: that we are his sons and daughters and he is our Father. We can be more that what we have become! The hunger in your heart is the desire to know God being a Father to you and to live in that relationship of love.

In the previous four chapters I hope I've provoked a response within your heart. I hope I've challenged what has become a 'normal' way of thinking or behaving. I've wanted to show that some of our fundamental beliefs are actually rooted in the tree of the knowledge of good and evil, rather than the tree of life. We have allowed ourselves to be driven by that subtle question, "what must I do?"

Trying to answer that question has led us away from the path of life and onto one of striving and performance. It has gently led us away from sonship into slavery and so eventually we realise we are running on empty. We are tired, drained and the life has gone from our heart.

As I have said, I've not written this book to judge but rather to provoke you into a different way of living. I hope it will nudge you out of complacency and into a search for the change your heart desires. We are recipients of grace, mercy and love. We are called to live in love and not the emptiness of servanthood. We have been born again in order to live a new life, to walk as

118

Jesus walked. To do so requires a heart transformation and that is what I have sought to describe.

In concluding this book, the final two chapters describe our sonship. They describe a profoundly different way of life to the one we may be used to. Yet, I believe they give us important keys to help us walk as Jesus walked.

Firstly, I shall look at comfort in some detail. When we are not comforted we build walls around our heart which lead to it becoming hard or closed. Walls lead to self-reliance and self-dependency where we become the centre of our life. Comfort allows the walls to come down and our heart becomes open to love once again. I am convinced that comfort is one of the most significant things that will cause everything to change in our heart.

Secondly, I shall look at weakness. Everything in our culture tells us that strength is good and weakness is bad. In the media, in politics, everywhere in society we constantly see strength and power being promoted. The apostle Paul, however, shows us a very different way: boasting in his weakness in order that the power of God may be seen. Jesus showed us the power of humility and total dependency on his Father. The secrets of the Kingdom have been hidden from the wise and learned and revealed to those with a childlike heart. It is to them that the Father is revealed (Matthew 11:25-27). Too often we have been taught to be independent and to rely on our own strength. That is one way to live but it is not the one Jesus showed.

This is a profound re-definition of how we have lived but it is one which will set our heart free. A comfort filled, dependent heart is what I believe we have been seeking. We may not be aware of it but far too often we have settled for the opposite which has worn us out. Eventually we come to a place where there is a longing in our heart for change. Out heart cry becomes, "there must be more than this!" And there is.

Change is within your grasp and when you embrace this new way of living from your heart, everything changes.

Chapter Nine

Comfort

There is an important topic for us to consider. In fact, I would rather not refer to it as a topic as that suggests it is something we need to understand with our mind. What I want to talk about is not something we grapple with in our mind, it is something we experience in our heart. It is therefore not a topic but an emotion, a powerful emotion that will change everything.

It is comfort.

I have discovered that we don't talk about comfort, let alone allow ourselves to receive and experience it. In one form or another, comfort is mentioned over one hundred times in the Bible and, therefore, it must be something that is very much on our Father's heart. To overlook something so important is a tragedy.

Comfort is a powerful emotion that brings healing to the deepest wounds in our heart. Let me start with the dictionary definition as I believe it captures the essence of what I will be addressing.

Comfort: to bring relief from pain, distress or affliction, to satisfy, to strengthen within. To provide a sense of wellbeing. Quiet enjoyment.

Comfort calms us. It restores us and brings us to a place of deep contentment. It is the catalyst for bringing our hearts into peace. Perhaps the word 'comfortable' is more readily understood. We like to be comfortable in our homes, with our friends or even in our favourite clothes. When we are comfortable we start to experience a sense of wellbeing where we can relax and let the internal walls of our heart come down.

As I travel, I find this is something that is not talked about let alone understood or experienced. We do not allow ourselves to be comforted and therefore we are unable to comfort others. In short, we fail to be the comforting people who will be able to welcome the broken world into our midst. For the church to be the nurturing family of God we need to be comforted. Like everything, it starts with us. We need to continually receive comfort ourselves in order that we can live from its surplus or overflow. Otherwise we are constantly striving to fill up our empty tank.

Before we start to look at comfort, let me take a look at the tragedy of being uncomforted.

"Again, I observed all the oppression that takes place under the sun. I saw the tears of the oppressed, with no one to comfort them. The oppressors have great power, and there was no-one to comfort them. So I concluded that the dead are better off than the living. But most fortunate of all are those who are not yet born. For they have not seen all the evil that is done under the sun." (Ecclesiastes 4:1-3 NLT)

Solomon writes these words at the end of his long life. As he looks back over his life his conclusion is stark: life without God is meaningless, whereas a fruitful life can only come from a life-giving relationship with our Creator.

Solomon sees people who have not been comforted and his conclusion is shocking. The dead are better off than those who have never received comfort. In fact, he goes even further. Those who have not been born are even better off because they have never had the tragedy of living a comfortless life. Solomon highlights how important comfort is and how much we need to discover the satisfaction and inner strength that comes as our afflictions are relieved.

We are not meant to live in a state of despair and brokenness. Such despair will lead to hopelessness and this is not the inheritance of sons and daughters. Receiving comfort should be natural for us and without it we will try to fill the hole with other things. For a time these things help but they are like a medicine - they relieve the pain for a moment, but as its effects wear off so the pain returns. This is not how we are meant to live.

As you continue to read this chapter can I encourage you to open your heart to be comforted. As you read, there may be areas of pain in your heart which the Father wants to comfort. He does not highlight these areas to condemn you but does so in order to bring you into greater freedom. Your heart will undergo a transformation as you are comforted.

Trauma

Trauma is something we all experience but it's something we experience in many different ways. We may try and cope, we may try and fight our way through it, or perhaps we even try to pretend that the traumatic event never happened which leads us to believe that really, we are ok. Ultimately, the only solution to the trauma we've experienced is for us to receive the Father's comfort.

Trauma leaves us feeling emotionally empty. We may be in shock, we may feel alone, abandoned, bereaved or rejected. Comfort is our only answer. I see our heart as a container and at the bottom trauma has settled like a heavy, immoveable weight. It may have been there for so many years that we have accepted its place in our heart. It may have become an unwelcome friend, but it has no place in our heart.

Comfort is a powerful expression of love which goes down the inside edge of the container of our heart. It goes right underneath the trauma. As we go on being comforted the strength of that comfort will gradually raise the trauma and, ultimately, lift it to the top of our heart. It can then float away and leave us free. Comfort is tender and kind, yet it is also strong and powerful. Strong enough to deal with any trauma we have experienced. Anything less will leave the trauma in our heart. It will continue to weigh us down and prevent us from entering our freedom. We will remain in distress and discomfort.

How much comfort do you need to receive? It cannot be quantified as you need to go on being comforted until you know the pain has been lifted out of your heart.

It may not be easy to face the pain. The good news is you don't need to face it on your own. Give Father permission to pour his comforting love into your heart. Allow yourself to go to the 'ouch' moment and then let him do the work of healing and restoration. We can't change ourselves. All we can do is simply receive the comfort he wants to pour into our heart. Remain in that place until you know you have been comforted, let it take as long as it needs to.

Mourning
Blessed are those who mourn, for they will be comforted. (Matthew 5:4)

We can lose our job, our possessions, our home, our income, our friends, our pets, our church or even the painful loss of a loved one. Loss often comes unannounced. It is always significant and it will affect us deeply. Although we all experience loss, I believe we don't fully understand the consequence of that loss either in us or in other people. Maybe we can empathise with the 'big' losses that others go through, but we don't appreciate the impact 'smaller' losses have because such things would not bother us.

A loss is a loss and we must be able to mourn our losses as this is part of the natural process of grief. Walking through grief is part of our healing process. If we are unable to mourn then the pain will remain buried in our heart, festering and producing bitterness and resentment. When we mourn we face what we have lost and in time our heart can be renewed. We are comforted. I particularly like how The Message paraphrases this beatitude.

You're blessed when you feel you've lost what is most dear to you. Only then can you be embraced by the One most dear to you.

Our mourning allows us to be embraced by the arms of perfect love. This comforting love is an expression of the Father's nature and personality and one we should receive daily.

As a mother comforts her child, so will I comfort you; and you will be comforted over Jerusalem. (Isaiah 66:13)

Mourning is not just about the big losses in our life; it is something we can do for every loss. As we discern our loss and allow ourselves to mourn we will have a deeper encounter with the Father's love. This transforming love will change everything in our broken, wounded heart.

Repentance and forgiveness
We find it easier to receive comfort for trauma and the losses we mourn. There is, however, another pathway to receiving comfort and that is through our repentance.

King David made a big mistake. He committed murder in order that he might commit adultery, which he then tried to cover up. Nathan, the prophet, confronts David with his sin. David could have Nathan imprisoned or killed but instead he allowed Nathan's story of the little lamb to lead him to repentance.

It is through his repentance that he was able to receive forgiveness and this became the doorway for him being comforted. It's the same for us. There will be times when we make a mistake (or several mistakes) and whilst these will inevitably have consequences they never prevent us from returning to the place of comfort and restoration. It is the pathway of humility that leads us to repentance and that will enable us to return home. Our Father does not reject us when we make mistakes but is always willing to welcome us back. Please note, there is a big difference between consequences and judgement. They are often confused as what we call judgement is more likely to be the consequences of our actions. Although forgiven and restored, we may still have to live with and deal with the consequences.

When we experience the comforting love of the Father through our own failings we are more able to have compassion on others when they make mistakes. Too often we judge others when we should forgive and comfort them; indeed this is Paul's exhortation for us:

If anyone has caused grief, he has not so much grieved me as he has grieved all of you to some extent—not to put it too severely. The punishment inflicted on him by the majority is sufficient. Now instead, you ought to forgive and comfort him, so that he will not be overwhelmed by excessive sorrow. I urge you, therefore, to reaffirm your love for him. (2 Corinthians 2:5-8)

As we forgive and comfort others they will be empowered to live from a free heart.

Father of all comfort
Paul had been beaten, shipwrecked, stoned and put in prison but we do not see any bitterness in his writings. In fact, what we encounter is the Father of **all** comfort. All the difficulties Paul had faced enabled him to write these words.

Praise be to the God and Father of our Lord Jesus Christ, the Father of compassion and the God of all comfort, who comforts us in all our troubles, so that we can comfort those in any trouble with the comfort we ourselves receive from God. For just as we share abundantly in the sufferings of Christ, so also our comfort abounds through Christ. If we are distressed, it is for your comfort and salvation; if we are comforted, it is for your comfort, which produces in you patient endurance of the same sufferings we suffer. And our hope for you is firm, because we know that just as you share in our sufferings, so also you share in our comfort. (2 Corinthians 1:3-7)

Paul is not writing about a theological concept but he is telling us of his own personal experience. He had been comforted. Comforted so deeply that he could forgive those who had persecuted him and his desire was that they would experience the same comfort as he had received.

This comfort is a free gift which I believe we can receive on a daily basis. It will set us free and make us whole. Comfort is not something we need purely for past hurts and wounds, it is something we need to enable us to live from a free heart. Instead of continually playing catch up, can you imagine what your life would be like if you constantly lived out of the overflow of comfort. Let us therefore look forward to a comfort filled life because, as we do, we will see how it changes everything.

Coming home

Comfort was never meant to be purely a sticking plaster for our past hurts. It is possible for us to build a surplus of comfort in our heart which will give us the reserves and resources to live more fully from our heart.

Our inheritance is to live as sons and daughters, to be filled with the Spirit of life and to live in peace and rest. My children do not have to do anything in order to be part of the family, they belong because they were born into it. We too are born into God's family, we belong and there is nothing more we can or need to do.

Living a comfort filled life will enable us to live in the fulness of this inheritance. We will discover that our lives are built on solid rock rather than on shifting sand. Our lives will be enriched and this will free us to enrich the lives of those around us. Living in love changes us and it also changes the people we meet. When we are comforted we know our heart has come home.

The latter part of Isaiah paints a big picture of the Father's comfort and, as we read, we see that redemption and comfort are closely entwined. Comfort really does transform our life.

The Lord will surely comfort Zion
and will look with compassion on all her ruins;
he will make her deserts like Eden,
her wastelands like the garden of the Lord.
Joy and gladness will be found in her,
thanksgiving and the sound of singing.
(Isaiah 51:3)

The barren and broken places of our heart become like a beautiful, fruitful garden. Instead of sadness there is joy, instead of emptiness there is fruitfulness. It is through the comforting love of the Father that we are transformed. I encourage you to meditate on this verse for a few moments. Allow the Father to pour his comfort into your heart. It really does change everything.

Reading through Isaiah 51 we see that, once comforted, we are brought home.

Those the Lord has rescued will return.
They will enter Zion with singing;
everlasting joy will crown their heads.
Gladness and joy will overtake them,
and sorrow and sighing will flee away.
(Isaiah 51:11)

A comforted heart finds its home with the Father. We are held in his eternal embrace and can know that whatever life may throw at us the joy of the Lord can fill our heart. We don't have to try and be joyful in difficult circumstances but we rest in his joy.

We see this homecoming in the story of the lost son in Luke 15. The welcoming embrace of the Father stopped the son in his tracks. He had no opportunity to deliver his pre-prepared speech trying to justify a place as a servant in his father's house. He was welcomed back. The son felt he had lost his sonship but so far as the father was concerned he had always been a son. Once welcomed home, the son knew he belonged. His heart was comforted in that homecoming.

Sadly, the elder son never experienced a homecoming. Although he had never left home, his heart was so full of bitterness and resentment that he did not know he belonged. He could not receive his father's comfort and so remained outside the house.

This is something we can only understand with our heart. When the Father comforts us he brings us home. All the searching and striving can fall away. The loneliness is taken away. We are home. We belong. We have found the place of contentment which so often alludes us.

Whatever our history or journey so far, we need a homecoming. This is not a one-off event but a lifelong journey where we experience the Father's affection at a deeper level. When I read John 15 I see two things: one is that we are meant to be fruitful and, secondly, that our fruit should last. For many of us this has not been the case. We do not feel we have been fruitful, or any fruit we have seen has not lasted. Our response is to work harder, trying to do more in our own strength in order to bring this fruitful life into existence. We end up with a life of performance and striving that wears us down and wears us out.

The homecoming I am describing will lead to us living from the overflow of a comforted heart. It is much more than simply receiving comfort for our past hurts but it's receiving (and going on receiving) comfort, in order that a reservoir builds up in our heart which will give us an inner strength. Our homecoming brings us into the place where we can receive. We discover the true reality of what it means to abide in Father's love. As we abide in his love, what we have previously strived for will become the natural flow of his life within us. We will start to see abundant and lasting fruit.

This is the overflow of a comforted heart.

We were never meant to be losers, always in need of a visit to the spiritual accident and emergency department. We are sons and daughters who have been set free to enjoy this life to the full (John 10:10).

This journey home is one of holiness. Too often we are put off by this word as it appears to be unattainable. How can I be holy? What do I have to do in order to become holy? How holy am I? These are the wrong questions as holiness is not something which can be quantified. We are already holy through the sacrificial and redeeming work of Jesus. We certainly can't make ourselves holy through our own effort. A comforted heart will be led in holiness because holiness describes the relationship we have with our Father. We cannot be truly holy until we have been comforted, as it is comfort which removes the shame and guilt from our life.

Our homecoming is not to scoop us out of and away from disaster. It is the outworking of our inheritance as our comforted heart finds its place of belonging in the Father's heart. We discover contentment.

Contentment
A lot of people are not content. They constantly seek new passions or desires, possessions or hobbies, activities or busyness. These things may not be wrong in themselves, but they will not bring ultimate satisfaction or contentment. When we seek these things we start to live under a constant pressure to have or to do more. A comforted heart has no desire to seek more, it is content.

King David shows us true contentment. Despite being the king of a large and successful empire he had discovered that contentment comes from a childlike simplicity and intimacy with the Father.

My heart is not proud, Lord,
my eyes are not haughty;
I do not concern myself with great matters

or things too wonderful for me.
But I have calmed and quieted myself,
I am like a weaned child with its mother;
like a weaned child I am content.
(Psalm 131:1-2)

As we live from the fulness of a comforted heart we will be free from fear. We will have confidence to try new things without the fear of failure. We will be more confident to be ourselves rather than constantly trying to meet other's expectations. A greater creativity will be released in us as we realise we are made in the image of the Great Creator. We will be free from shame, guilt and condemnation.

In Isaiah 61 there is a prophecy about Jesus. It is the same passage quoted by Jesus in Luke 4 when he read the scriptures in the synagogue. Although primarily about Jesus, this message will also be fulfilled through us as we live as sons and daughters.

If our heart has not been comforted there is no way we will be able to do anything contained in this passage. We may try and we will end up being exhausted or feeling inadequate. We simply can't give what we haven't received.

The anointing Isaiah describes is not for servants but for sons and daughters. It is for those who have been comforted by Father's love. It is for those who live out of the fulness of a comforted heart.

Comfort is a powerful expression of love. It heals, restores, brings us home and sets us free to walk as Jesus walked. It is something we don't talk about enough. It is certainly something we don't experience as much as we need to. As we are comforted and allow the reservoir of comfort to grow within us we will discover it changes everything.

Chapter Ten

Carried By My Father

Brothers and sisters, think of what you were when you were called. Not many of you were wise by human standards; not many were influential; not many were of noble birth. But God chose the foolish things of the world to shame the wise; God chose the weak things of the world to shame the strong. God chose the lowly things of this world and the despised things - and the things that are not - to nullify the things that are, so that no one may boast before him. It is because of him that you are in Christ Jesus, who has become for us wisdom from God - that is, our righteousness, holiness and redemption. Therefore, as it is written: "Let the one who boasts boast in the Lord." (1 Corinthians 1:26-31)

There is something in us that would like to be wise or strong. In reality, for most of us that is not the case and so we create the pretence of being strong or having it all together. The trouble is the pretence is easily seen through and our vulnerability all too easily exposed. We have been conditioned through our education system, through our politics and our workplaces that strength and self-sufficiency is a good thing and something we should strive after.

This is not what Paul is talking about in this passage. He is not preaching a message of how to be strong and independent but one of weakness and dependency on the Father. Despite all he'd been through he advocated a lifestyle of humility and weakness. This cannot be a pretence, it can only be the result of our heart being transformed. As his love becomes our security and resting place, the self-sufficiency and independence we have built up will start to fade away. God is not looking for the wise, the strong or the powerful. He sees through that pretence and looks for those who have discovered the power of weakness. We can create the illusion of strength. Weakness, however, is worked in us through adversity as we find our only answer is to be dependent on him.

However strong or wise we pretend to be, it is nothing when compared to his greatness.

Life can throw a lot at us. There are all sorts of pressures that come from our work, our health, our finances, our children or other family members. All of these come on top of and as well as the stuff going on inside our heart. There is pressure from without and within.

What do we do? How do we cope with all this pressure and pain? Do we let it govern us? Do we try and overcome these challenges in our own strength? Where do we run: into our own resources, strength and activity or do we run into the arms of the One who has already overcome the world?

I have told you these things, so that in me you may have peace. In this world you will have trouble. But take heart! I have overcome the world. (John 16:33)

138

He is the overcomer. Jesus, in saying these words, knows that we will face pressure or that we will go through internal struggles. But we do not need to fear because he has overcome the world on our behalf. What a relief! He has done what we are unable to do.

We do not need to try and become the overcomer. If we do it will be tiring and, ultimately, will lead to us being overwhelmed. There has to be another way, and there is.

In Genesis 32:24-32 we read the account of Jacob returning home after many years. He knows he is about to meet his brother, Esau, whom he had cheated and deceived. Their last meeting, many years earlier, ended with Esau threatening to kill Jacob, which is what caused him to flee for his life. Now he returns and, no doubt, is in fear of what the outcome might be. The night before they meet he sends his family and servants on ahead. He is alone, with God, in the wilderness. During the night he has an encounter with a man (whom he later realises is God) and this changes him. He wrestles with this man all night and refuses to let go until he receives a blessing. This encounter ends with the man touching Jacob's hip and putting it out of joint. From that day, Jacob walked with a limp as a permanent reminder of this encounter with God.

As you consider your own weakness you have to ask yourself if you are prepared to allow your pain and wounds to become a meeting place with the Father. As you allow this to happen you will be taken to a deep place. It's an encounter that can only happen in the wilderness, just you and the Father. It's not easy. It's an encounter where you have to wrestle with him; you fight for justice, healing and for freedom. It's a painful wrestle, but it leads to a deep awakening in your heart. Like Jacob, it will change you forever. You will carry the mark of that encounter with you for the rest of your life.

It's often said you shouldn't trust someone unless they walk with a limp. Why? Because their limp is a sign of humility, vulnerability and brokenness. Don't be afraid to walk with a limp. It is the sign of a depth that wouldn't otherwise be there. Your limp is an honest sign of weakness and dependency on the Father, brought about through an encounter with him. You cannot manufacture a limp. It is in our surrender to him that we are moulded to his likeness.

After the night wrestling with God Jacob received a blessing and names the place, Peniel. Alone, he had encountered God face to face. There is often no other way to experience the presence of God or to receive his blessing than through an encounter like the one Jacob had. Not easy, but it leads to us recognising and becoming aware of our own weakness and our need to totally rely on him.

It is through such encounters that we are renewed. We discover his strength empowering us and lifting us above our circumstances, However weary or tired we become, we can rely on his eternal strength which causes us to be lifted up as on eagles wings.

140

Do you not know? Have you not heard? The Lord is the everlasting God, the Creator of the ends of the earth. He will not grow tired or weary, and his understanding no one can fathom. He gives strength to the weary and increases the power of the weak. Even youths grow tired and weary, and young men stumble and fall; but those who hope in the Lord will renew their strength. They will soar on wings like eagles; they will run and not grow weary, they will walk and not be faint. (Isaiah 40:28-31)

The world wants us to be strong. We're told strength is good and weakness is bad. Yet as we walk with Father we discover the opposite is true. Weakness is good whereas our own strength will limit and restrict us. It will disable rather than empower us.

Paul had been able to accept his weakness. In fact, he not only accepted it, he boasted in it as he saw it was the key to the power of God being released. He also knew that weakness was a reality rather than a pretence. He had been forced into a position of weakness through circumstances and the various persecutions he'd suffered. He was not pretending to be weak in order to turn the tap of God's power on. He had become weak and it was through this state of his heart that God's power could be demonstrated.

If I must boast, I will boast of the things that show my weakness. (2 Corinthians 11:30)

I will boast about a man like that, but I will not boast about myself, except about my weaknesses. Even if I

141

should choose to boast, I would not be a fool, because I would be speaking the truth. But I refrain, so no one will think more of me than is warranted by what I do or say, or because of these surpassingly great revelations. Therefore, in order to keep me from becoming conceited, I was given a thorn in my flesh, a messenger of Satan, to torment me. Three times I pleaded with the Lord to take it away from me. But he said to me, "My grace is sufficient for you, for my power is made perfect in weakness. " Therefore I will boast all the more gladly about my weaknesses, so that Christ's power may rest on me. That is why, for Christ's sake, I delight in weaknesses, in insults, in hardships, in persecutions, in difficulties. For when I am weak, then I am strong. (2 Corinthians 12:5-10)

It is as we recognise and accept we are weak that we can open our heart to allow the power of God to flow through us.

For our heart to be transformed we will have to lay aside our pride and self-sufficiency and begin to rely on him. We recognise that we can do nothing in our own strength, that anything we do will either be a pretence or it will be limited to the extent of our own gifting.

Paul is also aware of the thing he calls a 'thorn in the flesh'. We don't know what it was for Paul but whatever it was had obviously become very frustrating to him. He pleaded with God for it to be taken away but that does not seem to have happened. He describes it as a messenger from Satan and, therefore, something which

142

was supposed to be destructive and distracting, something sent to steal his life. It was clearly not a blessing. Despite this Paul turns it round, he embraces it and instead of it being destructive it became a force for good. It enabled him to recognise and to be content with his own weakness. It is through his acceptance of weakness that he discovers the power of God being released through him. More than that, he finds strength through weakness (v10). God's power is perfected through the weak vessel of humanity.

As we understand this with our heart we see such a contrast to the way of the world, which constantly promotes strength. God loves to bless us and he will bless our activity but I believe his blessing will be limited to the extent of our achievement. Anything we achieve in our own strength is always going to be pretty minimal when compared to his immeasurable strength and power. As we become content with our weakness we will experience his power resting on us, and it is this that enables us, like Paul, to discern what true strength really is.

What do we do with our thorn? Of course we want to be free of it but more often than not it won't go away. Can we, like Paul, embrace our thorn and turn it round so it ceases to be destructive. Instead it can become the route by which God's power is released. If we are able to embrace our thorn as weakness then it will take the focus off us and our ministry, away from our productivity and allow us to rest in him. He becomes our resting place.

Embracing weakness is not natural nor does it come easily to us. Our tendency is to fight it and try to overcome it. We want to be victorious and somehow we think that overcoming our thorn is a sign of our great faith. Yet we see Paul embracing weakness and choosing to be dependent on his Father rather than trying to carry on in his own strength. I urge you to embrace your weakness and not to fight it. When you fight it, your energy is consumed and the focus is on the problem. Embracing weakness will take your eyes off the problem and you will start to gaze on the solution, who you will find to be your Father.

Whom have I in heaven but you?
And earth has nothing I desire besides you.
My flesh and my heart may fail,
but God is the strength of my heart
and my portion forever.
Those who are far from you will perish;
you destroy all who are unfaithful to you.
But as for me, it is good to be near God.
I have made the Sovereign Lord my refuge;
I will tell of all your deeds.
(Psalm 73:25-28)

When we are faced with the pressures of life, and the internal working of our heart, how are we going to react? When we recognise that we really can't do anything, and that we need to rely on him, we are brought to the same place as King David. Our dependency is built on the foundation of God being the strength of our heart, he is all we need. We may fail, our own resources may run out but God, our Father, is always there for us. His presence becomes our resting place. When we empty ourselves of self we embrace his sovereignty. It is only in that place of total weakness that we can say without any doubt, "God is the strength of my heart and my portion forever". The emptier we are of our own strength, the more real that statement will become to us. We will realise that we have come to the end of ourselves and it is in that moment we discover that we are being carried by our Father.

We all want to do things for God and to be used by him. I believe that is entirely natural and a consequence of us having given our lives to him. The problem is, this attitude can lead to us thinking that in some way God needs us. We think we are helping him out. That is so far from the reality of how it should be.

In Deuteronomy, Moses is reminding the Israelites of their history and their journey out of Egypt towards the Promised Land. It had not been an easy journey with many of the problems being brought about by the people's stubbornness and rebellion. However, Moses reminds them of the faithfulness of God, who despite their rebellion continues to be a Father to them.

Then I said to you, "Do not be terrified; do not be afraid of them. The Lord your God, who is going before you, will fight for you, as he did for you in Egypt, before your very eyes, and in the wilderness. There you saw how the Lord your God carried you, as a father carries his son, all the

145

way you went until you reached this place."
(Deuteronomy 1:29-31)

Even as the people are rebelling God reminds them that he is a Father. They do not need to be afraid, he has gone before them, he has fought for them and he has carried them all the way. This is the heart of our Father. We think he loves to carry our burdens, and he does. But he wants to do so much more than simply take the weight off our shoulders. He wants to reach down, pick us up and carry us as a father carries a child. This is a picture of intimacy and tenderness. It is not one of a father rebuking his rebellious children, it is an expression of a father's heart towards his sons and daughters. Despite everything, he wants to carry us all the way.

At the end of Moses' life we see a similar picture.

There is no one like the God of Jeshurun,
who rides across the heavens to help you
and on the clouds in his majesty.
The eternal God is your refuge,
and underneath are the everlasting arms.
(Deuteronomy 33:26-27)

Our God is mighty and powerful yet he surrounds us and carries us in his everlasting arms. A comforting picture of the tender embrace of our Father. We think it is all about us when really it's all about him.

In Isaiah 40, we read that God is not distant, nor is he angry, he does not judge nor hold our sin against us.

146

What does he do? He reaches down and holds us close to his heart, like a shepherd carries a lamb.

See, the Sovereign Lord comes with power,
and he rules with a mighty arm.
See, his reward is with him,
and his recompense accompanies him.
He tends his flock like a shepherd:
He gathers the lambs in his arms
and carries them close to his heart;
he gently leads those that have young.
(Isaiah 40:10-11)

Yet another picture of a strong and mighty God who, when it comes to dealing with his people, does so with love and tenderness.

As I read these passages I find myself asking the question: "Am I willing to be carried?" He will fight for us, he will defend us and so we can rest in his strength. We lean back in him rather than relying on our own effort. As we do, we discover that he is much more interested in loving us and carrying us than he is with any of our works.

I can no longer carry my children who are now all grown up, nor would they want to be carried by me! It is a small child that can be carried.

Jesus often demonstrated the point of his teaching with a child. In Matthew 18 the disciples ask Jesus who is the greatest in the Kingdom of God. I'm sure they were

147

expecting him to say that they were, after all they'd sacrificed so much in order to be with him. But it's not the disciples nor is it the wise and learned. It is those who come with a childlike heart and who are able to recognise their weakness and dependency on him. In fact we need a conversion. We need to stop walking in the direction we are going and we need to turn right around and walk in the opposite direction. This conversion will enable us to come as a child. And to do so, Jesus says, will require humility (Matthew 18:1-4). If we are unable to go through this conversion, this complete change of direction, then it is not possible for us to enter the Kingdom of Heaven.

It is to those with a childlike heart that the secrets of the Kingdom are revealed (Matthew 11:25-27). Those who have spent years trying to become wise and learned will find these mysteries hidden from them. It is the Father's good pleasure to reveal his secrets to those who know their weakness and vulnerability. In fact, it is this vulnerability which leads us to having a revelation of the Father. Jesus longs to reveal the Father to each and every Christian but it is only those with a childlike heart who will see it and who can enter this new relationship. This is offensive to many, I'm sure it was offensive to many of Jesus' listeners but it is the only way to discover the easy yoke of relationship as we enter our sonship and are totally yielded to him.

We are faced with a very important decision. We can carry on as we have been and where we seek to do everything in our own strength. Where our dependency is on our gifts and talents and our own limited abilities. Or, we can turn and become like a child, allowing him to reach down and carry us. If we allow him to do this he promises to carry us all the way. What a joy and relief that is! Through the difficult times and through the good times he will carry you. He never tires or becomes weary, he is more than able to carry you. He will take your burdens but he would rather carry you. He is more interested in you than he ever is with your activity. Sadly, we think it is our busyness which wins his heart. It's not, it's intimacy with him.

The decision I present to you is this: Are you willing to let go of your striving and goal oriented way of life? Are you able to let go of the managerial control so often seen in today's church and let him carry you? Can you be like Paul, who recognised and accepted that he was weak and could nothing in his own strength? Not only did he accept his weakness but he boasted in it because he knew it was through his weakness that God, the Father, was made known. In letting go and being weak, Paul saw he was strong, not in his own strength but enabled by the Father.

The pathway of weakness is new to us. It should be normal Christianity but sadly we have chased after being wise and learned. We have listened to the deceptive voice of the enemy, "Can God be trusted?" and so we have ended up trying to find an answer to the question, "what must I do?"

We will inevitably be faced with our weakness if we allow ourselves to be carried by our Father. We will be brought to the place of emptiness, knowing that the only way forward is to rely on him and to rest in his power. In that moment we also acknowledge his strength and we see that being carried by our Father is the best way. It is one filled with promise, hope and, above all, rest. Something we have earnestly yearned for we suddenly find. Our striving ceases and we become content.

Are you tired? Worn out? Burned out on religion? Come to me. Get away with me and you'll recover your life. I'll show you how to take a real rest. Walk with me and work with me—watch how I do it. Learn the unforced rhythms of grace. I won't lay anything heavy or ill-fitting on you. Keep company with me and you'll learn to live freely and lightly. (Matthew 11:28-30 The Message)

Our weakness is the key to the power of sonship being released in our heart. There is no other way. This is the way Jesus walked, it's the way Paul walked and, if we embrace it, it will become the pathway of freedom and life for us as well. It may not be easy but it is the only way your heart will be totally satisfied.

I believe there is an invitation for you to come. To come with a childlike heart and allow your Father to carry you. He promises to carry you <u>all</u> the way and as he does it will change everything.

Pause and Reflect

Before reading these two chapters I asked you to pause and reflect. I want to ask you to do the same now.

I believe you picked up this book because you want to see change in your heart. You have become dissatisfied with your current resting place and you know there has to be more.

The longing in your heart can be satisfied; there is more.

What we need is a re-discovery of the Father. Not simply knowing that God is a father or the Father but experiencing him being a Father to us. Once discovered, we can pursue his heart and the unfathomable depth of love that he has for us. A love that will never run out or give up but an eternal love that will continually flow into our heart through the Holy Spirit (Romans 5:5).

I have taken you on a journey. I hope you have been able to see that being a Christian is so much more than the guarantee of eternal life when you die. It is living today, tomorrow and everyday as a son or daughter to your Heavenly Father. I hope you have seen that the Father is after your heart rather than your activity. Anything we do for him flows from our heart of love for him. I trust you and I will be able to discover the good works which have been already prepared for us and when we do, we will be able to do them with all our heart.

151

I hope you have seen it really is possible to be rooted and grounded in love.

When I last asked you to pause and reflect I indicated I would show a profoundly different way of living to the one you may be used to. In these last two chapters I have written about two deep encounters of the heart. The power of a comforted heart and the power of weakness. Together they lead to the change you are seeking. Together they become the foundation on which everything is built.

The journey may not be easy. It will, however, be one that takes you into his heart in a way you've not yet experienced. It will lead you into the "more" that you desire and, yes, it will change everything.

And Finally....

For most of the past thirty years I have been involved in some form of church or Christian leadership. For nearly forty years I have been professionally advising many churches and Christian organisations. I have had the privilege of meeting countless people from many walks of life. I have spoken to and discussed issues with Catholics, Anglicans, Baptists, Evangelicals and all sorts of Charismatics. I've met people working with the homeless, those fighting drug abuse or addiction, people helping those in debt and others working in a variety of community based or social projects. I've advised mission organisations, those helping prevent human trafficking and many different churches. I've spoken in house groups, small village halls, school halls and church buildings of varying size, age and ornateness. I've been with young people, old people, single people and married couples. I've met poor, rich, educated and uneducated. I have been in churches in Africa, Russia, America, Canada and Europe.

All of the people I've met over these past few decades have had a few things in common. Firstly, they've all had a Christian faith. They have had an encounter with Jesus as their Lord and Saviour, they've had their sins forgiven and they knew their eternal destiny. They have a desire to please and serve him. They want to see change in their own lives and in the lives of those they are trying to help. The church leaders I've met and all those working for Christian organisations have wanted to see their work make a difference. They want individuals, communities and even nations to change as people discover the life changing revelation of salvation. Members of church congregations want to see the same change in their own life, in the lives of their family members and in their communities.

All of these people, from whatever denomination or organisation have a personal relationship with Jesus, many love the life of the Spirit and they all pursue something deeper with God.

All these people that I've described are part of the same family. Our family. There is an incredible diversity and wealth of experience in this family and it is one that should be celebrated at every opportunity. Of the main world religions, it is only Christianity that describes itself as a family. It is only Christianity that accommodates such a breadth of experience and has such an emphasis on a personal relationship with God. We truly are a broad church which, in the New Testament, is described as a family.

A family relates together, plays together, has fun together and yes, cries together.

But a family needs a father. This family lost sight of its Father way back at the beginning of our journey. We listened to the subtle lie of the enemy and so began a journey of independence and self-reliance. Instead of relying on a loving Father and trusting him to provide and care for us we chose to look after ourselves. In doing so, we have even ceased to care for other members of the family. Our faith is often more dependent on us than on him.

Although we lost sight of our Father he never took his eyes off us. At the end of Genesis 3 he did not change, we did. He did not have to try and find another plan, he stuck with his original one – to have a family.

In 1980 Thomas Smail wrote a very perceptive book called 'The Forgotten Father'. He says:

"To put the same thing another way, we have had in recent years a Jesus movement and a charismatic movement. The one has almost disappeared and the other is threatening to run out of steam, perhaps because each is in a different way inadequate to the gospel, which is basically a Father movement. It is not first a Jesuology (a doctrine about Jesus) or a pneumatology (a doctrine about the Spirit) but it is a theology or even a patrology – a doctrine about God the Father. It starts not with the cross of Jesus or with the gift of the Spirit, but with the Father who so loved the world that he gave his Son in his Spirit."

The danger, Smail says, is that an over emphasis on Jesus and the Holy Spirit (to the exclusion of the Father) will lead to us believing that God only has a functional relationship with the other members of the Trinity. If theirs is functional, why should ours be any different?

Probably one of the most revealing things Thomas Smail says is this:

"But as we look to Christ and the Spirit in their togetherness, we dare not forget the Father. If we do we shall see Jesus only as the one who faces in our direction, as Saviour, Healer, Baptiser in the Spirit, Renewer of the Church, who by his Spirit meets our needs for pardon, wholeness, satisfaction and self-fulfilment. We shall see the value of Jesus as his value to us rather than as his value to God. The charismatic renewal is in danger of becoming imprisoned in just such a man-centred, need-dominated distortion of the gospel where Christ and his Spirit can be easily reduced to the source of our blessings and the satisfiers and servants of our needs."

Wow! We have stopped allowing Jesus to lead us to the Father and instead made him the solution to our own needs. We have looked inward rather than to the Father.

My purpose in writing this book has been to help us rediscover what we have lost, or perhaps I should say **who** we have lost. As we discover the Father and his love for us we also rediscover our lost sonship. Our sonship is not functional, it is centred in a family with God as our Father and Jesus as our elder brother. It is a relationship that leads to life and life in it all its fulness.

A family needs a father and that is who God is. He does many things but Father is who he is.

Jeremiah 3:19 really does sum up the cry of God's heart.

156

How gladly would I treat you as sons and give you a pleasant land, the most beautiful inheritance of any nation. I thought you would call me 'Father' and not turn away from following me.

Why does he long to be called Father? Because that is who he is. The only relationship he ever wanted to have with his people is to be a Father, their Father. Indeed, this desire is fulfilled in a promise.

I will be a Father to you, and you will be my sons and daughters, says the Lord Almighty. (2 Corinthians 6:18)

This has to become the centre of our gospel message. God is not only the Father, he is <u>our</u> Father, <u>your</u> Father, <u>my</u> Father. He wants us to call him Father and to grow in sonship, the same sonship as Jesus. As we live as sons and daughters we shall see the doors of Heaven open as he releases the 'most beautiful inheritance of any nation' to us.

Yes, he is a father, he is the Father, but is he a Father to you? It is only as he become a Father to you that everything changes.

Afterword

Thank you James for writing the foreword and for your encouragement over many years.

I am very grateful to Julie Graham, who has done a thorough job in editing this book and correcting my many mistakes of grammar and punctuation.

And a big 'thank you' to my son-in-law, Rich, for designing the cover for me.

Here are details of other resources you may want to look at as you live in the Father's love.

A Father to YOU - www.afathertoyou.com
Audio and video teachings, teaching materials, inspirational videos and details of events in the UK.

The Father's Love Letter - www.fathersloveletter.com
An intimate message from God to you, in over 100 languages.

Fatherheart TV – www.fatherheart.tv
Inspirational videos and live webcasts to inspire and help you grow in the love of the Father.

If you would like to go deeper on this journey of love then I recommend books by James and Denise Jordan, Trevor Galpin, Barry Adams and Stephen Hill, all of which are available on Amazon.

Made in the USA
Middletown, DE
11 January 2020